Brewery
Operations

Vol. 3
Brewery
Operations

Practical Ideas for Microbrewers

Edited By Virginia Thomas

Brewers Publications
Boulder, Colorado

Thanks to Stephan K. Elliott, president of AMUS, Alpha Micro Users Society, Boulder, Colorado, for his assistance in typesetting this edition. His time and effort are greatly appreciated.

Brewery Operations
Vol. 3
Edited by Virginia Thomas

Printed in the United States of America
Published by Brewers Publications,
a division of the Association of Brewers
P.O. Box 287, Boulder, Colorado 80306 USA
Tel. 303-447-0816

Cover design by David Bjorkman,
David Thomas and Associates.

Acknowledgments

Special thanks to the following companies who assisted financially in the production of this book:

Adolph Coors Brewing Company,
Golden, Colorado

Anchor Brewing Company,
San Francisco, California

Anheuser Busch Brewing Company,
St. Louis Missouri

Buffalo Bill's Brewpub TM,
Hayward, California

F.X. Matt Brewing Company,
Utica, New York

Miller Brewing Company,
Milwaukee, Wisconsin

"A great pleasure in life is doing
what people say you cannot do."

Contents

Foreword

The fifteen chapters of this book are adaptations of the talks given at the fifth annual National Microbrewers Conference held in Portland, Oregon, on September 17 through 20, 1986.

As anyone who has ever had to put a remark into print knows, the American language is spoken very differently than it is written. With eye contact, a speaker is able to read his listeners' level of comprehension and decide to press a point, emphasize a previous point for reinforcement, or jump ahead skipping obvious steps of logic.

In editing these talks from the tapes made at the conference, I have made a conscientious effort to present each speaker's information while preserving the style and nuances of language that make each unique. Like a good beer, each speaker has his own distinctive characteristics. I've not watered those down.

Graphs and tables included here were faithfully checked against the originals to minimize error. My thanks to those speakers who allowed their charts to be used.

Virginia Thomas, Editor

1. Wort Production

Dr. Michael Lewis

Food Science, University of California - Davis
Davis, California

In order to produce consistent beer, you must have consistent fermentation. You must understand precisely what your yeast is, how it behaves, and how to handle it in a consistent and proper way. The same is true of the manufacture of wort. If are are going to produce a beer that is consistent and high quality, then it is necessary to produce that wort in a consistent and constant fashion. You must bear in mind, then, the variables of the brewing process. My talk today will address some aspects of the production of wort in a brewery.

One of the major passages of the brewing process is the conversion of malt into hopped wort. There are a number of processes that contribute to achieving that conversion. Milling is the very intense, very practical, very aggressive act of breaking up the grain. Mashing is the addition of water to achieve conversion. Lautering is the separation of the spent grain from the liquid wort. Kettle boil is a means of extracting the hops and stabilizing the wort. And finally, cooling is applied to the hopped wort, which can be pitched with yeast.

Wort Production

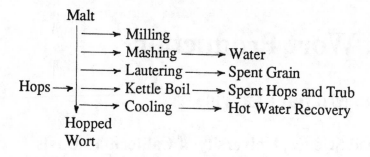

You can see that in this process water is input, and along with this, a proper temperature program is crucial. The outputs are spent grain, spent hops and trub, and the recovery of hot water in the cooling process. I will speak mainly about the mashing and lautering stages, a little about kettle boiling, and make some side comments about milling.

Wort production is largely a three-unit process that we can clearly identify. First of all, there is the unit process of **extract production,** which is essentially the mashing process. Next is the process of **extract recovery,** which involves lautering or the filtration process. Third, there is the process of boiling, which can be described as a unit process involved in **extract stabilization.** These are different events and have different requirements.

Extract production can be characterized as a biochemical process. It is a process that is biochemical because it depends on enzymes. Therefore, temperature is crucially and centrally important. Extract recovery is simply filtration, and is a physical process dependent on particle size and pressure. Extract stabilization is boiling. A physical-chemical process, it depends upon the input of heat energy, the transfer of heat energy from one side of a heat exchanger to another, and distillation.

We have, then, at least three different unit processes that occur in the brewhouse in a very short time. Let's look at these in more detail, and ask two pertinent questions about each of them: what needs to be done, and what are the agents of change?

Extract Production

In the mashing process, what has to be done? This has to be done: I have to convert the starch into fermentable and unfermentable sugars. I have to achieve the extraction of the alpha amino nitrogen that is contained within the malt and that was put there by the maltster, God bless him. And I also have to extract the flavor and color of the malt.

How then shall I achieve this? What are the agents of change? First of all, in terms of direct extraction, I'm concerned about water, especially wetting the malt and the achievement of solution. So these are the agents of change. The water has to be of a certain kind, has to be of a certain temperature, and has to have a certain length of contact. It is not insignificant to consider water as an agent of change in the mashing process. After all, the wort we produce will be 90 percent comprised of water.

Another agent of change, and a crucially important one, is the action of enzymes. Enzymes are the agents that actually do the work of converting starch into fermentable and unfermentable sugars.

The temperature program we choose, or lack of a program, is going to be another central agent of change. Consistent handling of these agents is necessary for consistent wort production.

What can go wrong? With what results?

Extract Recovery

Extract recovery is primarily the process of lautering. What has to be done? First of all, our objective is to separate the liquid from the solid to produce a lear wort. The clearer we make the wort, the more likely we are to achieve a successful final fermentation. This is a function of brewhouse design and operation.

We are also trying to achieve a high yield. This may be somewhat less important for microbrewers and pub brewers than it is for large-scale breweries. The importance is that you make money out of the yield. At the same time, you cannot afford to spend too much time in the brewery running off the wort. You wish to achieve not only a high yield and a clear wort, but also to achieve it rapidly. This is also true in the microbrewery. There is nothing more miserable than standing around waiting for a lauter to run off.

We have two additional factors which are often set aside: diffusion, as a means of achieving extract yield, and viscosity, as a variable in the run-off from the lauter.

Another agent of change is the particle size; this influences the way in which the lauter runs, and therefore needs to be thought about, controlled, and understood. The relationship between particle size, viscosity, diffusion, and recovery has to be clearly understood.

There is also the function of bed depth. The depth of the bed is a variable in the way in which your lauter can be run. In large-scale industry, of course, in order to achieve rapid runoff, the bed is widely spread and is shallow. Such vessels are expensive because a wide, shallow bed involves lots of manufacturing. Most microbreweries have a much smaller vessel, meaning a much deeper grain bed depth. This vessel is cheaper, stronger, more easily constructed, more easily run, and takes up much less space.

Another agent of change is the pressure drop from the top of the bed to the outlet into the grant. That is the hydrostatic pressure that influences the pull on the bed.

These agents, then, also influence the consistency of wort production.

Extract Stabilization

The third unit process is extract stabilization. What has to be done? Wort stabilization has many aspects, three of which are the destruction of enzymes, the precipitation of protein, and the sterilization of the wort.

Flavor adjustment also has many aspects. The most obvious are the extraction of the hops, the isomerization of alpha acids into isoalpha acids, and the distillation of hop oils during the course of boiling. But there are many other flavor adjustments occurring. If you were to put no hops at all into boiling wort and taste the distillate, you would be astonished at the amount of undesirable volatiles that are being steam distilled out of the boiling wort.

Finally, the concentration of wort is another objective of the boil. You evaporate excess water off the wort as a part of the kettle boiling process.

Heat and steam distillation are the agents of change, and a full, rolling boil. Full, rolling boil is the way in which the brewer describes the kind of boil that is necessary to achieve these things.

These agents influence consistency.

Extract Production

Let's go back and pick out some of the key elements that make these operations go. To start with extract production: if you were to pick out a centrally important item in the mashing process, it would be the control of temperature. Temperature is the key to success, because extract production is 90 percent the result of enzyme action on relatively insoluble substrates.

In other words, the material isn't particularly soluble. Although the maltster has converted the barley into malt. He has not necessarily rendered the starch (which makes up 60 percent of the malt) instantaneously soluble. So we must first make this material soluble. In the second event, the enzyme action has to be sufficiently rapid to work, and the enzymes have to be sufficiently conserved during the mash.

The mash must be hot enough to dissolve the starchy substrate. The way in which this substrate dissolves is related to malt modification. If the malt is very highly modified, as in the old, traditional, English kind of malt, the starch will dissolve easily. If it is undermodified, a higher input of heat energy will be required to dissolve the substrate.

The mash must also be hot enough to promote rapid enzyme action. Some enzyme action will occur in the mashing process at almost any temperature, but to make it react rapidly, the mash should be as hot as it can tolerate. Yet it must also be cool enough to ensure sufficient enzyme survival. We cannot make the mash so hot that the enzymes are instantaneously inactivated. If we do, the starch will not be converted. We must make the mash just the right temperature.

At the end of the mashing process, there is little point in having enzymes left over, so we run the mash as fast as possible. That means as hot as possible. Then, at the end of the process, the enzymes that were in the malt are more or less inactivated. The mash should be hot enough to affect the substrate, hot enough to make the enyzmes act rapidly, but cool enough to ensure sufficient enzyme survival.

If you have a lower diastatic power, that is, if you have a lower content of enzymes in the malt, then you must mash at a lower temperature to ensure that enough enzymes survive during the mashing cycle. If you have a plethora of enzymes, then you can drive the mash at a higher temperature. Please note the interrelationship among mash temperature, malt modification, and the content of enzyme in the mash.

Extract Recovery

Particle size is, in my view, one key to success in extract recovery. In lautering, extract must be run off from between the particles, and diffused from within the particles that make up the grain bed.

Malt particle size must be small enough to permit proper extraction of wort, and small enough to form a filter bed on which the wort may be clarified during filtration. Particles must also be small enough to permit rapid penetration of water, and small enough to allow outward diffusion of extract to occur rapidly and easily. The particles must act as a filter bed to clarify the wort. The particles themselves make up the filter bed, not the slotted bottom. Clarification takes place in the bed of material itself.

The malt particles must also be large enough to permit satisfactory percolation through the bed, and to provide resistance to bed compaction. The particles must be small enough to meet the above requirements, yet not so small as to obstruct the runoff of liquid. It's a balancing act. In microbrewing, with relatively deep lauter beds, larger particles are preferred over smaller ones.

Extract Stabilization

A full, rolling boil -- adequate heat transfer -- is the key to successful extract stabilization. Brewers always speak of "full, rolling boil." I remember walking through the AnheuserBusch brewhouse in Fairfield with the brewmaster. Suddenly his brewer's ear told him that the kettle was at a simmer, not a boil, and he immediately asked that the heat on the kettle be turned up. But operators often won't run at a full boil because the hot liquid might splash out of the kettle.

I repeat, a full, rolling boil is the key to success in extract stabilization because it promotes physical and biological stability, evaporation, and flavor adjustment. The boil should be vigorous at all times in order to promote the following actions:

Protein aggregation -- a small, but important amount of protein is removed by the kettle boil, and a rapid boil is necessary for protein precipitation;

Hop extraction -- hop extraction and isomerization take place, and the full vigor of the boil is necessary to ensure (whether you use pellets or hops) that there is a full and active motion of the hops within the boiling wort to promote maximum solubility;

Sterilization -- a full, rolling boil assures that there is adequate circulation, adequate sterilization, and enough energy;

Wort concentration -- the full boil enables us to get adequate evaporation of water;

Removal of volatiles -- steam carries with it a whole range of compounds that you wish to get rid of from the boiling wort;

Flavor development -- this includes the extraction and isomerization of the hops, and also the development of new flavor and color compounds based on the boiling process.

I have a friend in Britain who says that the process of brewing is the process of removing from the malt everything that's undesirable. If you smell-taste the condensate that comes off the kettle, you will understand that the steam that's coming off is carrying much more than water. The steam carries off the volatile compounds you don't want in the finished beer. They may not have a particular aroma in wort, but when the yeast has acted on them during fermentation, they produce a highly unsatisfactory character, among which are some of the sulfury compounds.

But the heat exchange surface should not be too hot, to avoid burning the wort. In some forms of heat transfer surfaces, the wort is actually burnt, which makes it impossible to produce a pale beer. If your objective is dark, heavy beer, then the kettle boil is one place where you can develop those characters.

In summary, in all three of these operations, it is a matter of conducting the process with the correct balance between the good, the possible, and the bad.

Three Types of Mashing Systems

If you look over the traditional mashing systems used in the world today, you can find infusion mashing, decoction mashing, and the so-called double mashing, which is the American system of mashing.

The infusion mashing process operates at a single temperature, by definition. It also uses a single vessel, which is a mash-lauter. The infusion mash is an unstirred, stationary mash.

Decoction mash is a temperature-programmed mash. The temperature program is achieved by boiling roughly one-third portions of the malt mash and then adding them back to the malt mash to raise its temperature. The process is a multi-vessel system, and in order to achieve efficient heat transfer, it is a stirred system.

In the double-mash, the temperature is achieved by the addition of boiling adjuncts to the malt mash. The rice or corn is boiled and then added to the malt mash with vigorous stirring. It is a multi-vessel process.

Now let's look at the advantages and disadvantages of these systems. As I look at this list of three possible systems, I judge the infusion system as being a highly desirable choice for many microbreweries, and certainly for pub brewers.

Advantages

First of all, the infusion system requires fewer vessels than any of the stirred systems. The mash tun, which is a traditional term for the mash mixer, also acts as a lauter vessel. It performs in a single vessel two of the unit operations we've been discussing: extract production and extract recovery process.

Stirring and mixing are not required in an infusion mash, so you are saved the cost of buying stirrers and mixers. Similarly, you do not have a temperature program or heat input devices and their controls. Temperature control is easily achieved by controlling the temperature of the hot water that goes onto the malt. Given sufficient experience, you can hit the right temperature every time.

American malt is well adapted to the infusion system. Microbreweries -- and certainly pub brewers, who usually do not use adjuncts that necessitate a multi-vessel system -- would do well to consider this system first. It has a number advantages in cost and simplicity of operation.

I've shown the infusion system in the drawing below. There are only two vessels in the brewhouse. First there is a mash-lauter. From there, the wort is run into a kettle-whirlpool, then through a cooler.

If you decide to use an adjunct or a temperature program, you are faced with having a multi-vessel system, as shown below. There must be a mash mixer with a stirrer, and (for adjuncts) a mash kettle or cereal cooker, which

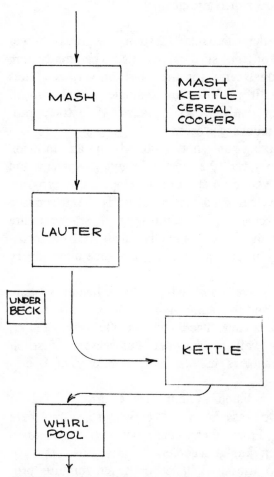

DECOCTION OR DOUBLE MASH

supplies boiling material into the mash mixer. The mash then has to be dropped down into a lauter vessel, and because the mash has been vigorously stirred, a sophisticated lauter vessel is necessary to achieve filtration -- a wider, shallower vessel.

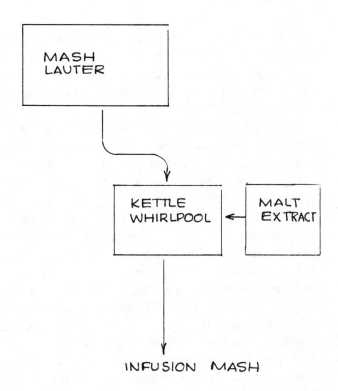

Disadvantages

The disadvantage of the infusion system is that it has relatively low productivity. There can be only one brew in the brewhouse at a time, and it may be possible to brew only one brew per day. There may be some difficulty in chasing brews through the plant, one after another, but for most microbrewers and pub brewers, this is not a major problem.

If it is, you must double up the system, or go to a multivessel system. In going to a more complicated system, such as using an underback, for example, which is an extra wort holder, as many as three brews can be in the brewhouse at one time. And that is the main advantage of the multi-vessel system: it allows you to chase brews through the brewhouse with far more efficiency. Thus, the potential productivity of the multi-vessel brewhouse is greater than the productivity of the two-vessel system, but you should pay for that advantage only if you can use it.The two-vessel system is cheaper, simpler, and conceptually easier to operate than the multi-vessel system.

As an aside, I want to comment on syrup brewing. Some people have said it can't be successful, but syrup brewing can make excellent beers. To undertake syrup brewing, you need only a kettle-whirlpool to build a brewhouse. It is the ultimate in simplicity, because you have given much responsibility over to the syrup manufacturer. Instead of mashing the malt, you simply dilute the syrup into the kettle-whirlpool. Then, if color is desired, you simply add a small side tank with a simple run-off device to extract crystal or black malts with hot water, without any particular temperature program. This system allows the production of different products from a single source of pale syrup. It is a very useful strategy for pub brewers, and indeed, for many microbrewers.

Mash-Lauter System

Let me preface this discussion of a mash-lauter system by reminding you of two things I've already said: you need satisfactory temperature control for proper enzyme action, and adequate particle size control for satisfactory extract recovery.

Temperature

If I were to conduct a series of individual infusion mashes in my mash-lauter at different temperatures, and then measure the extract achieved, I'd get low extract from low temperature mashes. Why? The starch does not dissolve easily, because the temperature is too low for the adequate solubilization of the substrate. But if I were to use progressively higher temperatures in this series of tests, I'd reach the point where the starch was successfully dissolving and the extract adequate. Only at very high temperatures would the extract start to drop off. The point is, temperature influences the amount of extract produced in an infusion mash, simply by its affect on starch solubility.

If I were now also to measure fermentability, that is, the amount of extract that can ferment, I'd see a different relationship. Very low temperatures, where very little extract is dissolved, will produce very fermentable extract. As I go up in temperature, the fermentability decreases, and at the stage where the enzymes are heavily inactivated, the fermentability of the wort severely drops off. Why? Because the enzymes are intensely sensitive to excess heat.

Here are two opposite actions caused by temperature: extract goes up with increasing mash temperature and fermentability goes down. Only a comparatively narrow range of temperature produces good extract **and** good fermentability. That is the "brewer's window." It's where the

brewer balances the achievement of adequate extract with
the achievement of sufficient fermentability.

The temperature of the brewer's window is a function of
the amount of enzyme in the system and the solubility of
the substrate. In other words, it is not a fixed number.
It depends on the kind of malt being used and the kind of
wort being made. We might say that the range of temperature in the brewer's window might be 62 to 65 degrees C.
This applies to a malt with a low diastatic power that is
very well modified. This is typical of the kind of malt
originally designed to go into a mash-lauter in the old
days of English infusion mash.

But that temperature would almost certainly be substan-
tially higher if I were using American malt, which has a
higher diastatic power. I can then go to a higher temperature because I have more enzymes. And I need to go to a
higher temperature. because the substrate is less well
modified and hence less soluble. So the brewer's window
becomes 65 to 68 degrees C or even higher.

The brewer's window can be moved in relation to the
kind of wort being produced. If I want a more highly fermentable wort, I move the window downscale a little. If I
want a less fermentable wort, I move the window up a little. But if I move the window accidentally or ar-
bitrarily, I will influence the amount of total extract
and the amount of fermentable extract, with dire conse-
quences for wort and hence beer consistency.

Particle Size

Visualize for a moment a mash-lauter with a very deep
grain bed to get some sense of relationship between particle size and runoff. When the mash has finished, there

are large particles of spent grain contained within a wort substrate. The wort (extract) is inside the particles as well as around them.

At runoff, the wort is first drawn from between the particles. Then the next stage occurs. Here the sparge water has entered the grain bed, and has penetrated halfway down. Below the level of penetration, the wort is still the same as it was in the first stage, and the particles still contain the wort.

When the sparge water enters the grain bed, the particles still contain extract, but now in a sparge-water environment. By diffusion, they now give up most of their extract. With excessive exposure, however, they may then start to give up undesirable proteinaceous, tannic, and starchy materials.

The last stage of runoff occurs when the original wort has exited the lauter and sparge water covers the particles and begin to exit the lauter. The particles at the surface of the lauter have given up all their desirable extract, but particles situated lower in the lauter still hold desirable material. The sparge must therefore be continued to recover this.

The design of the lauter vessel has to consider this sequence of events. The first draw must be slow; if that first viscous, dense wort is drawn too aggressively, it will collapse the bed. You can begin to draw more rapidly when there is less dense wort remaining in the bed; and finally, when the wort is essentially gone, the rate of lautering can be raised, because only thin sparge water remains. This last stage should be rapid to avoid drawing undesirable extract from the grains.

At the same time you need to reach a satisfactory end gravity so that you efficiently recover the maximum amount of desirable extract.

Let me develop this idea in more detail by looking at two designs for mash-lauter. If one design uses wide, numerous slots and large particles, the energy or suction of the drawn wort is dissipated over a relatively large area, and there is a low negative pressure at the slots. The bed is less likely to collapse and clog the slots.

However, in a design with narrow slots and fine particles, the energy transmitted to the bed is much greater. There is intense negative pressure, which is likely to pull down the bed.

Vessels for a large brewery generally use small particles, narrow but numerous slots, and a very shallow grain bed to get good runoff. In a mash-lauter for a microbrewery, it is necessary to have a different concept. The grain bed is generally deep, and therefore the slots should be as large and as numerous as possible to minimize the pressure on the bed. This allows for very rapid runoff, so you don't have to sit around biting your nails and wondering if the bed is going to collapse.

Brewery Sizing

Brewery sizing is crucially important. For a microbrewery, production capacity is the only constraint. In a brewpub, there are many constraints dictated by space, location, flexibility requirements, appearance, etc.

Design to Succeed

Finally, I want to make a few cautionary comments. First, please do not "design for failure." People who do this think, "If it doesn't work, I don't want to have invested too much money."

Design for failure usually shows up in the size of the plant; in inadequate, used equipment; in skimping on technical advice whether it be a lawyer, accountant, or brewing consultant; and in building in cheap square footage in a poor location.

Then there's the idea that quality sells itself. Quality sells, but it does not sell itself. Many brewers feel that quality will cause customers to beat a path to their door, but it isn't true. There are many, many fine beers in the world today that don't sell well due to the brewer's naivete, lack of business experience, and lack of marketing savvy. I'd rather see people with tremendous business experience and proper capital entering the microbrewery business that those whose experience is technical only.

Dr. Michael Lewis is a professor of brewing science at the University of California, Davis, Department of Food, Science and Technology. He teaches courses on the various aspects of brewing. He is also a consultant to the industry, a designer, and a builder of small brewing plants.

2. Cottage Brewing

Robert McKechnie

Granville Island Brewing
Vancouver, British Columbia

Four years ago, I was comfortably ensconced as a university professor at the University of British Columbia. I had summers off, Christmases off, Easters off, long weekends off. The most difficult thing I had to do was phone the bank occasionally and make sure my paycheck had been deposited. My life was pretty comfortable. Then the phone rang.

"Hello, McKech, this is Bill Harvey," the voice said. "Do you want to build a cottage brewery?"

"Sure," I said.

That was the start of what have got to be the most interesting, exciting, and scary four years of my life. When I began four years ago, my hair was a nice, even brown without a trace of grey -- and look at it now. I want to tell you about those four years.

Granville Island Brewing is now up and running profitably -- although we certainly had some problems getting to that stage. Today, I'll tell you the story and point out some of the things we learned in the process.

The Team

I'll start by talking about our team. Bill Harvey is an idea man. About fifteen years ago, he was wandering around a slummy industrial area in downtown Vancouver called Granville Island, when he came across a warehouse with a "For Lease" sign. He saw the potential in that warehouse, and promptly took out the lease on it. Then he gathered friends and associates with money to start a restaurant there. Now, over a decade later, Granville Island is a flourishing, attractive part of the city. Most of the industry there has been replaced by shops, restaurants, pubs, and theaters.

In 1982, Bill Harvey was traveling around the world when he saw a little brewery in Santiago, Chile, that sold fresh, unpasteurized beer. He fell in love with the idea and said, "If that's going to work in Santiago, it will work back home."

Every team has to have men of vision -- but they are rarely known for their organizational ability. Bill is no exception. He talked the idea over with Mitch Taylor, a friend and an astute businessman. Mitch had come up through the ranks at Imperial Oil, becoming one of their youngest vice presidents. He has been on his own as a businessman/entrepreneur for the last fifteen years, and has been involved in the Granville Island renovation project -- building a marina, starting a yacht club, and importing boats from Taiwan. He and Bill tossed the idea of a brewery around, decided it was worth pursuing, then proceeded to assemble the team.

They asked Ian Robertson, a lawyer, to come aboard. I knew he was a really good lawyer because he had an office in the corner on the top floor of a skyscraper. He has been an invaluable member of the team, dealing with all the legalities involved in financing, starting, and operating a brewery.

Another team member was Ted Reichgeld, a general contractor who had worked with Mitch in developing the Granville Island area. I guess we could have hired a contractor, but Ted was brought onto the team because Mitch's approach is to involve people to heighten their participation.

Larry Sherwood is our marketing man. He was formerly the marketing director for McDonald's in western Canada, and was brought onto the team to do the marketing study, and oversee how the beer would be packaged and sold.

I was brought on to do the technical work, build the plant, put the pots and pans together, help select the brewmaster, etc. I'm not sure why I was chosen. At the time, I had had considerable experience on the consumption end of a brewery, but I didn't know anything at all about making beer. I think the reason was that they had tried other friends, weren't successful, and were getting down to the bottom of the hectoliter. The other reason was that they knew I had a sabbatical year coming up from the university and they could get me cheap.

Notice that none of us had any brewing experience. That might seem strange -- but at that stage, we had no money, and were unable to hire a brewmaster. No one wanted to give up his job at a brewery to come work with a bunch of guys with only an idea.

But we did have the major bases covered with our team. We had a businessman who knew his way around financially, a lawyer, a marketing man, an idea man, and a technical man. If I were giving advice on starting a brewery -- or any business -- I could end my talk here. If you get the

right people on the team, you'll do okay. Our success is
due in a large part to having competent professionals on
our team.

Developing the Idea

Once we had the team in place, we sat around and drank
all sorts of beers as we planned the brewery. Within two
weeks, we had worked ourselves into a lather of euphoria.
As our enthusiasm grew, we knew we were going to make
terrific beer and people were going to pile into our
brewery and heap money on us. Then we actually began to
put our plan into effect -- and that's when the real fun
and learning started.

By far, the most significant task was raising the
money. We had a little seed money -- about $25,000, which
was necessary to get us through the stage of raising our
real money. But before we could begin approaching people
with our idea, there were some important questions that
had to be answered.

How Much Money?

The key question in raising money is, how much? First,
there are capital costs -- one-time costs such as building, equipment, etc. Second, there are operating costs
incurred on a continuous basis such as raw materials,
electricity, wages, etc. Then there are revenues, which
relate to when you think your product is going to get on
the market, how fast you'll build sales, and how much
you'll charge for your beer.

There are numerous unknowns here, e.g. cost of equipment, interest rate, sales, etc. The way to handle these

is to build a financial model. We estimated our capital costs, building costs, renovation costs, equipment costs, operating costs, and on and on, then built a financial model of the operation on a spreadsheet on a computer. If you don't know what a spreadsheet is, or Lotus 1,2,3, then you're not doing your financial homework. My advice to you, then, is get someone on board who does. This is of absolute vital importance to your business.

We built the spreadsheet, with all its variables, then projected our cash flows on a month-by-month basis. In the beginning stages, we knew we would be making huge capital expenditures. We figured our operating costs would occur six months later. Then we planned for the stage when we thought we'd be in production and getting some revenues. This was an invaluable tool for us.

The next step, after building this computer model, was the hard one. All the variables in the financial model are just that: variables. For example, the price of malt. You plug in the price of malt, which was $450 Canadian for a metric ton in 1982, and your computer model shows your costs and revenues and how much capital you need. If you change the figure to $475, the model reflects that. We played a lot of "what ifs" in finding out what our brewery was sensitive to and what it wasn't. We looked very carefully at the variables that would greatly affect the brewery.

It is very, very difficult to predict costs. In retrospect, I have to admit we made some bad mistakes. We took a very good, sound, professional approach and developed a very nice working model, but many of the numbers we put in were not realistic. Buildings costs were pretty accurate because Ted had had a lot of experience doing renovations, although we did go over some due to requests by the city.

But equipment and installation costs were really only uneducated guesses because none of us had ever built a brewery before. We got a bit of help through visits to River City Brewery, Sierra Nevada Brewery, Independent Ale Brewery, and Anchor Brewery , but we were really whistling in the wind at that point. All we could do was plug in our best estimates, realizing that it entailed an element of risk.

In the planning, we hoped to find a used bottling machine, and I went to see several. There was one we could have had free, but it would have cost too much to renovate. And it couldn't be properly cleaned. Since our game plan called for an unpasteurized beer, we couldn't afford any risk of contamination. So we bought a new machine. In retrospect, that was a good decision, but it threw our financial model out of whack.

The item that really threw us, however, was our projected beer sales. We figured we'd begin to get revenues about six months from financing, and that was true. We had projected the size of the brewery to be 5,000 hectoliters a year, but we made a big mistake. We assumed that if we had a 5,000-hectoliter-a-year brewery, we'd sell over 400 hectoliters each month (5,000 divided by twelve months).

We had fallen so in love with our beer that we thought people would be buying it continually throughout the year. We knew there was seasonality to beer sales, but we chose to overlook that fact. It was a very bad mistake, which has had severe financial repercussions ever since.

We cranked out maximum production during the summer, and we were selling out of beer. Then the rains came in September, and lasted until the following June. Our beautiful beer sales dropped to half, and there was nothing we could do about it, as we didn't have the money to do any media advertising.

As a result, we didn't have anywhere near the revenues we predicted. The bottom line of all this was that by underestimating our equipment costs and overestimating our revenues, we found ourselves nearly $1 million short by the end of the first year. That discovery made for interesting times.

One important lesson we have learned is that generally speaking, you get one kick at the financial cat when you raise money. You can't go back to the investors at this point and say, "We've got a really good thing going here. Now all we need is another $1 million, and things will be fine."

Nor are the banks very approachable at this stage. They are much more likely to be thinking that it is time to pull out of the project entirely before it goes under.

We were very, very lucky and managed to survive this financial crisis. I think the main reason was because we had done everything so professionally and had produced a beautiful little brewery that everybody liked. We were able to say exactly what had gone wrong financially and why. With a very honest, open approach, we managed to keep the banks on our side, and in fact, they lent us more money.

We explained the situation to our suppliers as well and were able to get some interim financing and stretch out the accounts payable. And finally, we were lucky because one of our directors was able to reach into his own pocket and help out considerably.

My advice is to build a good model, get accurate figures by listening carefully to people with brewery experience, and then provide a large financial cushion to fall back on if things don't go as planned.

How to Raise Money?

You can borrow money, and you can raise money through equity by selling shares. You have to decide how much you'll borrow versus how much you'll realize with shares. We thought fifty/fifty was appropriate. The more you borrow from the bank, the more you retain as owners. But then, you're also paying more interest, which cuts your profitability.

We needed $1.5 million, so at fifty/fifty, we planned to raise $800,000 by selling stock. In approaching investors, we put together a nice, professional prospectus. We even included a little section on beer and brewing, showing a picture of malts and people laughing and drinking beer with a big head. I included a flow chart for brewing beer, Larry put in a section on our marketing plan, and Mitch had a business plan.

We began flogging the plan. We'd invite people over, have a table full of imported beers for them to try, and some hors d' oeuvres. We'd give our little dog-and-pony show, and then go to the back of the room and wait for people to come and write out the checks. But it didn't happen that way. We gave our presentation over and over, but about the only thing that changed was that we started by serving potential investors lobster and shrimp and in the end, we served pretzels and peanuts.

People are not as willing to part with their money as you might think. They ask questions. They asked us if our idea had ever been done in North American, and our answer was no. They asked if we had brewery experience. Our an-

swer was no. They asked what the tax advantages to them
would be. Since we had set up the business as a regular
corporation, there were none.

After several such dog-and-pony shows, all unsuccessful
in acquiring checks, we made the big decision to restructure to a limited partnership, where the investors had
all the tax writeoffs for the first couple of years. If
they bought a $25,000 unit, they picked up $12,500 in tax
advantages. To make a long story short, soon after doing
that, we raised the money.

Marketing

We did not go into business with any preconceived marketing ideas, so we needed to ask questions about what
kind of beer we'd make, how we'd sell it, and how much
we'd charge for it. These were difficult questions to answer. The marketing man poured over reams of statistics
to find out how much beer was produced in British
Columbia; how much was bottled, draft, and imported; how
much was lager and ale; and so forth. He did a lot of bar
hopping, talking to bartenders, and asking how much people would pay for beer. He rode around in beer distribution trucks, did many blind tests, conducted focus
groups. From this came his marketing plan.

We realized there was a strong general movement toward
highquality products versus mass-produced, low-quality
items. There was a sentiment against big business, and a
movement toward small, low-tech, high-touch business.
People can come in and talk to us, tour our brewery, get
a taste of beer. As a policy, we do not use the term
"microbrewery" to describe ourselves. We are a cottage
brewery. Why? Because "micro" sounds like microchip or

microprocessor. It sounds high-tech. But we want an intimate, high-touch image, so we prefer the term "cottage."

That kind of thinking carried through to our packaging. We talked about PET bottles at one time. Although we liked them, they would have destroyed our image because they are massproduced. We chose to go with old-fashioned, tall-neck bottles.

I won't speak about the engineering, except to say that I think we did it reasonably well. I made a few mistakes, but they weren't too serious. The most important decision we made was to buy a Krones bottling machine. It cost a lot, but it has been marvelous. There is absolutely no contamination in the beer, and hardly any oxygen pickup.

We went first-class in the plant. We didn't buy brand-new, shiny equipment in every instance, but bought used equipment as much as possible. I didn't do what one little brewery did: I was in England scouting a used-equipment dealer when I ran into a secretary of a brewery who had been sent to buy tanks. That brewery is now gone.

My point is that I like used equipment, but you have to have someone who can judge whether it is capable of doing what you want it to, and whether it is in good condition. I was able to make those decisions for our brewery, and saved considerable money in doing so.

We also saved money through my designing the equipment I couldn't find used: tanks, refrigeration systems, piping, etc. But I wouldn't have done that if I had not had a technical background. I'd buy new equipment, package systems, or I'd hire an engineer.

We brought in a German brewmaster, which was part of our marketing plan. We had decided to do an unpasteurized German beer, and therefore we hired a real German brewmaster, with a nice German accent, and had him meet the public on television and at functions.

In conclusion, once we were up and running, we went through some tough financial times; but we did things professionally, and managed to keep our heads above water. We've now increased capacity up to about 12,000 hectoliters a year, and our sales curves are going up nicely. I'm pleased to report that we've been in the black for about the last four months, and it looks like we're going to stay that way.

Dr. Bob McKechnie is a founding partner of Granville Island Brewing in Vancouver, and Upper Canada Brewing in Toronto. As such, he completed the engineering for each brewery and tended all the technical matters until the brewmasters were hired. He is also head of R.E. McKechnie and Associates, a company which specializes in mechanical engineering design and development.

3. Comments on Brewing

John Young

Young's Brewery
London, England

It's a great, great privilege to be here. The last time I was speaking at a function, the microphone wasn't very good, and there was a lot of rustling at the back. I yelled out, "Can you hear me in the back?"

A voice answered, "Yes, I can hear you all right. But if there's anyone who can't, I'm very willing to change places."

The Spaniards, who are noted for their bullfighting, have a saying about after-dinner speeches: It's a point there, and a point there, and an awfully lot of bull in between.

Anyway, if I may address you, greetings, my fellow crusaders. I believe that's what we all are. We are the defenders of quality and taste; we are responsible for the resurrection of good beer, by producing superbly crafted beers as they really used to be. And we must bond together for the common purpose of providing an alternative to the routine commercial beers of the giant mega-companies.

For too long they have dictated to the consumer and brainwashed him with advertising. In England we have an

actor called John Cleets, who has a funny walk; you may
have seen him on the Monty Python show. Only recently
he's been shown in an ad for Budweiser, which is very
good, but why shouldn't he speaking for an English beer?
In the commercial, he says that English ale is dark so it
conceals the tadpoles. Well, John Cleets may be a very
good actor, but he knows little about beer.

Our brewery began 300 years ago, and it's been Young's
Brewery for 135 years, since 1831, when my great, great,
great grandfather took it over. I'm the sixth generation
of Young to run the brewery, and I have a son.
Thirty-five years ago, we, along with many others, were
imperiled by the invasion of big, American-type, megacom-
panies with their carbonated products. Thirty-five years
ago in England, there was a Mr. Watney brewing at Watney's. There was a Mr. Younger brewing at Younger's.
There were several Courages brewing at Courage's. There
was even a Mr. Bass brewing at Bass.

All that has been swept away now, and replaced by accountants. There are no more Watneys, Youngers, Basses in
the business. This is an important development for all of
you and all of us. Many of the smaller family breweries
went under, and it was they who provided the quality and
the closer connections with their customers, which is so
important.

I think one of our secrets of success at Young's is
that we have always given our head brewer complete free-
dom to purchase the finest materials, the best hops, and
the best malts. Not everyone has done this.

At the time of the beer revolution thirty-five years
ago in England, there was also a revolution in the bakery
trade. There were once a great many small bakers in England, like your microbreweries now, which made the most

super bread that was full of taste and texture. Then the
big flour millers came along, and grabbed a great deal of
the market. When the standard of living rises, however,
people eat less bread, and when this happened in England,
the flour millers were in trouble.

But, enterprising as they were, the flour millers per-
suaded many brewers in England to brew not with malted
barley, but with wheat flour. Mr. Watney fell for this. I
can remember tons and hundreds of tons of wheat flour
going into Watney's brewery. Thankfully, Watney's brews a
much better beer now than they did then. But most of the
little bakers were squeezed out, and we had the emergence
of horrible plastic bread, with which you are all very
familiar.

I have three French friends, and you know that no one
cooks better food than the French. My three friends were
taking the train from Dover up to London and were looking
out the window. The first one looked at the green, lush
hop fields and said, "What marvelous country."

The second one saw the many gardens and said, "How
beautiful it is!"

And the third one said, "Thank God, they can't cook
it!"

Brewers were once very slack in looking after their
beer once it had left the brewery. But care for the quality of a beer doesn't end at the brewery gate. It's important to follow up on the beer outside and see that the
good qualities are kept up. Draft beer especially was not
always well looked after. I recall many British pubs
where you couldn't get a decent pint -- which may have
been part of the reason we were overtaken by carbonated
and pasteurized beer.

I once when into a pub and, upon receiving a half pint

of beer, exclaimed to the barman, "My goodness, this beer's terrible!"

He replied, "Don't you complain. You've only got a halfpint. I've got seven barrels in the cellar."

I think we all share a great advantage in being small. In England we have a phrase circulating now that "small is beautiful." We must exploit that. Big business gets too topheavy. Do you know the story of the two fleas climbing up the elephant's leg? The mother flea said to the little flea, "The bigger the organization, the bigger the balls at the top."

We should also exploit the tradition of brewing quality beer. In our brewery, we have stuck to the tradition of having horses, like Budweiser. We have an eight-horse hitch that we use for showing, but we still follow the tradition of delivering beer by horses. Our teams still deliver fifty tons of beer a day to the local pubs around the brewery.

We also have a mascot called Ramrod (a ram), because Ramrod is our trademark. One day the vet came to us and said, "I think your horses need a little music to cheer them up." So we installed some music down in the stable, where Ramrod and the horses are kept.

The first time they started up the music, Ramrod dropped down dead. When I heard this, I rushed down to the stable and asked why.

"What do you think the first tune was?" the stable man asked. "There'll never be another youuuuu (ewe)."

Another story about that is I came home rather tired one day from the brewery and laid back in my armchair near where my wife was doing the crossword puzzle in the evening paper. She suddenly looked up and said, "Darling, what is a word for a female sheep?"

I said, "You." And that's how the fight began.

But she got her own back again the next day. I came back very late and was actually quite sober, so it was unkind of her to say, "Darling, drinking makes you look so handsome."

"I haven't been drinking," I said.

"Ah, no," she said. "But I have."

Anyway, I was told to make my speech short tonight. Someone once told me that if you haven't struck oil in five minutes, stop boring.

When I finished the last after-dinner speech I gave, I asked, "Was that okay?"

"My God," they said. "You were like a British Rolls Royce: well oiled, could hardly hear you, and thought you were going on forever."

Thank you very much. It's been a tremendous pleasure.

John Young is president of Young's Brewery, Wandsworth, London, England. The breweries products are Bitter, a soft, complex beer; Special, with a malty finish; Ramrod, with a smooth balance between bitter and malty; Young's Export Special London Ale, with its floral bouquet; and Old Nick, a classic dark barley wine.

4. Liefman's Brewery
Madame Rose Blancquaert-Merckx

Brewmaster
Oudenaarde, Belgium

When I was asked to speak here, I felt uneasy about it because I am not a good speaker. Now that I am here in front of you, I feel even more anxious. I can make good beer, but maybe not good speeches.

I am from Oudenaarde in Belgium, a very small, nice country in Europe that is situated between France and Germany. There are about ten million people in Belgium, outgoing people who like to communicate and visit. There is a great deal of culture in Belgium, but most of all, there is very good beer. We are famous for our traditional Belgian beer.

The annual production of beer in Belgium is about 12 million hectoliters, 79 percent of which is bottom-fermented beer. There are now 120 breweries left in Belgium; yet in 1900, there were over three thousand. Still, the production now is nearly the same as it was then, although it is mainly concentrated in the big breweries who took over the smaller ones.

It seems a pity to me that the small breweries disappeared. At the turn of the century, nearly every village had its own brewery, many of which brewed their own unique, specialty beer. Those good beers are now gone forever, and I'm very glad that didn't happen to my beer. Our brewery has been in existence for over 300 years, and my wish is that it can go on for another 300 years.

I began in the brewery as a secretary. I didn't know anything about brewing, but my boss, who was a very clever man, liked to go on holiday, and had no one to make the beer when he was away.

One day, he told me, "I'm going to teach you to make beer so I can go away more often."

So from then on, I learned how beer is brewed -- although I often did things I didn't know the reason behind. Then suddenly, my boss died, and there I was, alone with the brewery. The family asked me to go on brewing, or the brewery would have had no worth, and I did. That was sixteen years ago. And the beer is still good.

I have always had a very good sense of taste, which I think is important for a brewer to have. You can learn how to make beer without being an engineer (this is especially true in my brewery, since we don't use any chemicals), but you do need a good sense of taste to be able to blend beers.

I taste the beer twice a week at 11 a.m. This is the time when a brewer has the best sense of taste. I taste ten or twelve beers to know which ones are ready. Every brew is different, although I don't know why, since each is made in the same way. One is sharper, another more full-bodied, and you have to blend them to get the good, all-round taste you like and need for consistency.

I would never sell a beer without tasting it myself; if I couldn't taste it, I wouldn't trust it. I know that in large breweries there are various methods for tasting, but I believe that you also have to drink it to know how it tastes when you swallow it. I don't believe in sipping.

In Belgium, we mostly sell our beers in cafes, where people come to drink and socialize, although they are somewhat different than the pubs in England. On my trip to the United States, I haven't seen many cafes, while in Belgium, they have always been plentiful. There are fewer now, but those that exist are nicer, more luxurious. Belgians frequent cafes often, and often stay there visiting and drinking until 5 a.m.

In the cafes are found a number of very special beers: Trappist, gueuze, dark ales, etc. There is plenty of variety in Belgian beers. I make four kinds of beer -- all dark ales, which I can't compare to any that you might know. I make them dark because in Oudenaarde, where I live, dark ales are a traditional kind of beer called "Oudenaarde beer." Beer has been traditionally named for the area where it was brewed, just as beers produced in Antwerp or Louvain are called "Antwerp beer" and "Louvain beer."

In the past, beer was sold mostly in the area where it was brewed, but since so many small breweries have closed, our beer is sold throughout Belgium and also exported to The Netherlands, France, Italy, Switzerland, Canada, and a little to the United States -- which I hope will increase.

Our beer is still made in the same way it was 300 years ago -- which may seem unbelievable, but it is true. Our production process is a long one, compared to other breweries. When I brew, I begin at seven in the morning, and continue until the beer goes for yeasting the next day in the late afternoon. The beer stays in yeasting for about five days, then goes to lautering in the tanks for five, six, or eight months. Then it is kegged or bottled in Champagne bottles that are liter-and-a-half magnums, wrapped with foil. They are very nice looking.

Our brewery is comparable to a microbrewery, not to big breweries which seem like clinics -- they are so full of buttons that run the machinery that controls the beer. We really work on the beer and take care of it. When I brew, I watch the beer from the moment it begins until it leaves the brewery. I have to taste it several times in the process, until I determine that it's good enough to sell.

I make four kinds of beer. Ordinary beer is one, which we send to cafes and supermarkets. It is 50 percent young beer mixed with 50 percent old beer, or "Golden Band" beer.

"Golden Band" beer is meant to be stored three, five, ten, even twenty years in the cellar, until it tastes like wonderful, fine wine. It is about 5.6 alcohol by volume. Michael Jackson has kindly called it one of the best brown ales on earth.

Another of our beers is cherry beer, which may seem strange to you. Once a year, in July when the cherries are harvested, I buy 50,000 kilos of a very special kind of cherries. They are very dark, very small, but very, very tasty. I buy them without the stalks, but with the pits left in, and put 12 to 15 kilos of cherries into the tanks of beer with a special sugar for six to seven months.

Every month I taste the cherry beer to see how it is progressing. The cherries must be left just long enough so that all the fruity taste and cherry essence go into the beer and only the pit and skin are left. Yet, they cannot be left too long or the beer will pick up the oily taste of the pit, and also the foam will be ruined from the oil. Our cherry beer is different than any other in Belgium because it is not made on a base of gueuze (a spontaneously fermenting beer).

Lately, we have also added raspberry beers to our list of products.

Earlier I mentioned that a brewer needs a good sense of taste. But to make beer, he also needs patience and more than anything, a caring love for the beer. This is one of my strongest assets.

Now my two sons help me in the brewery -- Olaf, an engineer, and Manuel. With them, I feel confident that our brewery can go on. We make the beers in a very ancient and traditional way, but I'm not going to change.

Our process is very labor-intensive. The brewing is in copper, which is very messy to clean. In fact, there is as much cleaning going on in our brewery as brewing. But as long as I live I will brew in the same way, and I believe I will always be able to make good beer.

Madame Rose Blancquaert-Merckx is Brewmaster at Liefman's Brewery in Oudenaarde, Belgium. Aside from her love for brewing, she has a great interest in sports, music, and dancing. She is a member of the supreme council of the "Chevalerie de Fourquet" and also of Zonta.

5. Yeast and Fermentation

Earl L. Van Engel

Blitz-Weinhard Brewery
Portland, Oregon

One of the biggest problems in brewing beer is achieving uniformity, and most of the problems that thwart that goal are not mechanical, but biological. To successfully maintain your business, you must maintain control over the biological functions that occur during production. Fermentation can make or break your product, so this is an area where you need solid knowledge and expertise. Today we'll cover the microbiological control of yeast during fermentation.

History of Yeast Discovery

First, in taking a short look at the history behind modern microbiology, we see that the very roots of this science began with Anthony Van Leeuwenhoek, of Delft, Holland. In 1676, Leeuwenhoek wrote a letter to the Royal Society of London describing the microscopic world of organisms for the first time. Among those, he identified yeast.

Appert, in 1831, was the first to stabilize beer by

deepheating. He is known as the father of the canning industry.

Louis Pasteur, however, is the father of the science of microbiology. During the years 1855 to 1860, he researched the fermentation problems of the French wine and beer industry. He also worked with British brewers, showing them drawings of the lactic acid bacteria and cocci that were problems in their beers. It was Pasteur who proved that yeast produces alcohol during fermentation.

It was in Denmark in 1883 that Emil Christian Hansen isolated the first pure cultures of yeast and began using them for the manufacture of beer. Then in 1935, Danish workers Winge and Lausten discovered that the spores produced by yeast were of a sexual type with Mendelian characteristics.

In 1943, Carl Lindegren at Southern Illinois University first identified the spores produced in Ascomycetes as having different mating types.

Brewing Yeasts

Ascomycetes are yeasts that produce spores, called asci, inside their cells. This process is called meiosis. Growth by budding during fermentation, which does not result in a change or reduction in the number of chromosomes within a cell, is called mitosis. Saccharomyces typically produces four spores of two mating types. Then as the cell wall ruptures, each spore forms one cell with one set of chromosomes called haploids. One of each mating type fuses to reform diploids, cells with two sets of chromosomes.

Probably via natural selection, the yeasts used by early brewers were those that were strong fermenters, i.e., yeasts that fermented wort most vigorously and produced beers with desirable characteristics. Since then, it has been found that most of these yeasts, whether ale or lager yeasts, are polyploid, meaning they have more than two sets of chromosomes.

However, most brewing yeasts have lost their ability to sporulate, possibly a result of their polyploid nature. Therefore, sporulation is a good test to determine if the yeast you are using has brewing yeast characteristics.

The two kinds of yeast used in brewing today are Saccharomyces cerevisiae and Saccharomyces uvarum. S. cerevisiae is primarily used in ale fermentations. It is a top-fermenting yeast described as being hydrophobic, and rises to the top at the end of fermentation as it traps carbon dioxide. S. uvarum is said to be hydrophyllic, and settles to the bottom of the fermenter at the end of fermentation.

Important Yeast Characteristics

There are probably as many differences within the lager-yeast category as there are differences between the lager and ale yeasts. The primary fermentative difference between a lager and an ale yeast is that lager yeast, S. uvarum, ferments melibiose (a disaccharide), while ale yeast, S. cerevisiae, is also baker's and winemaker's yeast.

Differences in yeast flocculation at the end of fermentation are also important to brewers. Most good brewer's yeasts flocculate. If your yeast doesn't flocculate, but remains in suspension, there is poor recovery and the beer becomes more difficult to filter. If the yeast flocculates too early, and rises or settles before the beer has finished fermenting, an excessive amount of unfermented sugars may be left in the beer.

Metabolic characteristics are also important to the brewer. Anaerobic metabolism during fermentation produces carbon dioxide and alcohol and makes beer. However, brewer's yeast needs a strong respiratory system. A yeast without a good, normal respiratory cycle will probably produce off-flavors in beer. During glycolysis, glucose enters a ten-enzyme (EMP) system to produce pyruvate. In the presence of oxygen, the pyruvate forms acetyl CoA (CoA meaning co-enzyme A) prior to the formation of carbon dioxide and water by means of the tricarboxylic acid cycle and the cytochrome system.

Glycolysis Plus Respiration (Growth)

Sugar -- EMP cycle -- Pyruvate -- Acetyl CoA --
TCA cycle -- H_2 Cytochromes + O_2 -- CO_2 + H_2O +
Energy (15 Units Equiv.)

During a respiratory or growth cycle, the yeast generates an excess of energy, necessary for growth and lots of heat.

Glycolysis Plus Fermentation (Intramolecular)

Sugar -- EMP cycle -- Pyruvate -- Acetaldehyde -- CO_2 +
Alcohol + Energy (1 Unit Equivalent)

In brewing, if we continually aerate the pitched wort, we end up with carbon dioxide and water and not with beer. We must aerate the wort at the start of fermentation, and then let the yeast ferment the wort to produce carbon dioxide and alcohol via yeast pyruvate and acetaldehyde.

Brewers are fortunate that most good brewing yeasts sporulate poorly. Subsequently, they do not produce all the genetic variations that sporulating yeast do during meiosis and recombination.

Fermenting power is also important, but more difficult to measure. The Carlsberg Breweries in Copenhagen have fermentation cylinders for comparing the fermenting activity of one yeast with another. Different brewer's yeasts may ferment at different rates of speed under uniform oxygen, nutrient availability, and temperature.

Mutation -- A Yeast Problem

In the brewing process, the brewer is pitching about 15 million yeast cells and harvesting 60 million cells. Under natural conditions, for every 1 million cells there is one mutant. Most are not important, since the mutant yeasts compete with normal cells during fermentation.

However, some genetic inclusions that are carried in the cytoplasm (among these are elements of the cytochrome system) can be harmfully effected by copper, dyes, or improper laboratory procedures. As a result, yeast cells can become respiratorydeficient, producing high levels of diacetyl or 4 vinyl guaiacol.

Flocculation can also be lost or changed through improper laboratory procedures.

Excessive residual amounts of diacetyl in beer is one of all brewers' biggest problems. To help control this problem, brewers need a strongly respiring yeast -- one with a good, complete cytochrome system. Respiration can be measured very simply with special media that contains indicator dyes.

The formation of 4 vinyl guaiacol in beer is another offflavor compound produced by mutant brewer's yeast. All wort contains phenol compounds, one of which, ferulic acid, is produced in large amounts during mashing. Some yeasts possess a decarboxylase enzyme that converts ferulic acid into 4 vinyl guaiacol.

This compound produces a phenolic, spicy, clove taste in beer, and is a yeast-related problem. A good brewer's yeast produces good clean beer, where the esters, the hops, and the lack of abnormal notes are clearly evident. Yeast-related offflavors are easy to eliminate: all you need to do is change your yeast. Better yet, test your yeast when you start to make sure it is what you want.

Yeast is not a sacred cow; if you have a faulty yeast, by all means change it. If you have a good brewing yeast, then by all means take care of it. At Blitz Weinhard, we use the same yeast over and over again.

During fermentation, glucose, maltose, and triglucose are absorbed through the yeast's cell wall, and hydrolyzed to form alcohol and carbon dioxide. It has been reported that yeasts may lose their ability to hydrolyze the trisaccarides (triglucose) and leave about 15 percent of the extract unfermented. This leaves a sweeter, wortier-tasting product. If you encounter this problem, this may be the reason.

Very little appears in the literature about brewing yeast's abnormal sulfur metabolism, but some sulfur compounds in parts per billion produce some very unpleasant, noticeable notes. One simple test for abnormal sulfur metabolism is noting the odor of the gases yeasts give off during trial fermentations. Do they smell clean? A very mild sulfury odor is normal because of the sulfur compounds all yeasts produce during fermentation. Strong off-odors may show up in the beer.

Controlling and Testing For Mutant Yeasts

If your brewery does not have a complete lab, the best way of testing for mutants is by odor and taste. If you are running into problems with diacetyl, 4 guaiacol, or the formation of abnormal sulfur compounds, you can test for them using different yeasts in laboratory fermentations.

To avoid these problems, you need to maintain your own yeast. Get it from a reliable source, and then take care of it. You can prevent a great deal of trouble with proper handling.

To maintain your yeast, boil and cool some wort and inoculate it with your pure yeast culture. Let it ferment for a week or so at cool temperatures. After two weeks of refrigeration, decant off the beer and reinoculate the yeast into fresh, sterile, boiled wort using aseptic technique. Keep repeating this process.

If you want to use a media for growing and maintaining your cultures, use MYPG, a mixture of .3 percent malt extract, .3 percent yeast extract, .5 percent peptone, 1 percent glucose and a little over 1 percent agar for solidifying. Transfer your yeast to fresh, MYPG agar slants every six months, allowing them to stand at room temperature for one day before refrigeration.

Other Yeasts of Importance

Saccharomyces diastaticus is a yeast that produces glucoamylase. This enzyme functions outside the cell, breaking down a beer's dextrins to simple sugars that can be transported into the cell. This yeast also has the ability to produce the dicarboxylase, which forms 4 vinyl guaiacol producing a spicy, clovelike flavor in beer.

Saccharomyces pastorianus yeast forms elongated cells and creates problems with off-flavors and hazes. S. pastorianus is one of the organisms used to produce gueuze and lambic beers. Although an acquired taste in Belgium, these sour beers taste spoiled to us.

Schwaniomyces yeast also produce a glucoamylase that breaks down dextrins and is being tested for the production of low calorie beers.

Killer yeasts, also known as zymocidal yeasts, produce protein toxins that kill other yeasts. Even small numbers of killer yeasts can destroy all the brewer's yeast during a fermentation. Many of these yeasts also produce enzymes that are diastatic and break down dextrins in beer.

New Advances

Spheroplast fusion is the primary method being used today to transfer desirable genetic characteristics from one yeast to another. The cell walls of the yeast are dissolved with an enzyme produced by snails. This exposes the cell's cytoplasm, and permits the transfer of spheroplasts from one type of yeast to another.

Currently, work is being done on transferring the enzymes that break down dextrins for the production of light beers; improving amino-acid biosynthesis to limit the production of diaceytl precursors during fermenta-

tion; infusing brewer's yeast with killer yeast characteristics; etc.

Yeast-cell immobilization is another relatively new
idea for brewers. How practical this would be for large
breweries is questionable, but it might have a future
with the microbreweries. In this process, yeast cells are
immobilized on calcium alginate gels to make a solid mass
of yeast in a matrix. The wort is run through the matrix
and the yeast ferments the beer. After a few months, the
matrix is discarded and replaced with another, fresh one.

Yeast Management

In the brewery, yeast selection is a foremost consideration and is often accomplished through trial and error.
As previously mentioned, get your yeast from a reliable
source. Different yeasts produce different end-products
and flavors. However, to a great extent, beer flavors are
affected by the environment and fermentation procedures
rather than by the yeast. A primary goal of every brewer
is to use a yeast that produces clean beer and ferments
well.

Beer odor and taste and yeast flocculation and
sporulation characteristics are all factors that need
examination. To test for sporulation, inoculate a
vigorously growing yeast onto an agar slant of 1 percent
potassium acetate. This media enhances yeast sporulation.
After three to five days of incubation, smear some of the
yeast onto a glass slide, heat fix and stain it. Use a
water-saturated solution of malachite green. Leave the
stain on the slide for ten minutes, rinse with water, and
counterstain for thirty seconds with safranin. The spores
will stain blue green.

Fermentation

The primary goal of fermentation is to optimize all conditions so that the fermentation will proceed as rapidly and as uniformly as possible. Speed and consistency are imperative. During the first several hours of fermentation, there is a lag phase. At this point, the yeast is taking up oxygen and nutrients for its use in developing enzymes to grow and to ferment the wort.

Active fermentations should take approximately three to five days, depending on the percentage of extract and temperature, and proceed in a linear fashion. Fermentations that take longer usually indicate a problem. Fermentation conditions may not be optimum, and the fermentation may not proceed to completion. Once the fermentation stage has finished, a good practice is to let the temperature hold for one or two days so that the yeast in suspension can properly end-ferment the beer and remove any undesirable compounds -- particularly alpha-acetolactate, which is the precursor to diacetyl.

Then the temperature of the fermenter should be dropped as quickly as possible. This preserves both the fermented beer and the yeast. Then yeast that has flocculated should be harvested and used again as rapidly as possible.

During fermentation, the yeast goes through a typical growth cycle beginning with a lag phase. In this phase, the oxygen is absorbed from the wort. The glycogen that has been stored in the yeast cells during the stationary phase is utilized as a source of energy so the yeast can produce unsaturated fatty acids and sterols that are vital for cell-membrane formation and the transport of

Chart A

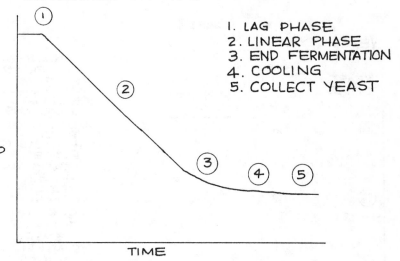

CONVERSION OF WORT TO BEER

1. LAG PHASE
2. LINEAR PHASE
3. END FERMENTATION
4. COOLING
5. COLLECT YEAST

Op

TIME

nutrients during the active phases of fermentation. These lipids accumulate primarily in the cell membrane near the cell wall. There are also lipid reserves within the yeast cell itself.

Once the lag phase has been completed, the yeast grows in a logarithmic phase during which the fatty acid and sterols that have been developed are diluted and passed down into the daughter cells. During brewing, there is normally a threeto fourfold increase in the number of cells.

Following the lag phase, the yeast undergoes a stationary phase in which yeast cells both die and are formed at about the same rate. During the latter stage of the stationary phase, as the fermentation is reaching its conclusion, the cells produce glycogen as a reserve energy source that will be used during their next growth cycle.

Chart B

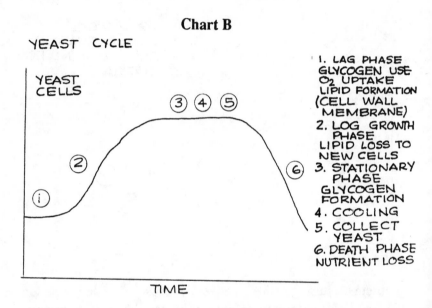

YEAST CYCLE

YEAST CELLS

TIME

1. LAG PHASE
GLYCOGEN USE
O_2 UPTAKE
LIPID FORMATION
(CELL WALL
MEMBRANE)
2. LOG GROWTH
PHASE
LIPID LOSS TO
NEW CELLS
3. STATIONARY
PHASE
GLYCOGEN
FORMATION
4. COOLING
5. COLLECT
YEAST
6. DEATH PHASE
NUTRIENT LOSS

At the end of fermentation, the yeast should still be in the stationary phase when the cooling is turned on. Refrigeration is necessary for the yeast to survive until it can be used again. Long, protracted fermentations, or fermentations where cooling is not available, result in excessive glycogen utilization and cell death, which produce a poorer, weakened yeast crop.

The most vigorous fermentations, which should be goal of all brewers, are accomplished when the yeast is turned over from fermentation to fermentation as rapidly as possible so that the yeast is in its most viable, active condition.

Factors Affecting Fermentation

There are many factors that affect fermentation. The yeast being used should be pure, have a good flocculation characteristic, have a strong respiratory system, have good fermenting power, and be well maintained. A list of equipment and a number of procedures that should be used in evaluating production yeast are given below.

Some Basic Laboratory Equipment

Microscope, 400 X, lamp
Slides and cover slips
Neubauer Hemocytometer
Capillary pipets
Dropper bottles
Hand tally
pH meter
Buffers pH 4 and 7
Cylinders
Hydrometers
Thermometers
Propane torch
Inoculating needle
Lens and blotting paper
Graph paper to plot fermentation curves
Brewing library

Flocculation Test

1. Place several heavy drops of sedimented or skimmed yeast on a glass slide.

2. Gently flood the slide with tap water.
3. Disperse the yeast with a finger so it produces an
   even, moderately light, milky haze in the water.
4. Tilt the slide back and forth for 30 seconds to one
   minute, bringing the cells in suspension in contact
   with one another.
5. Note the degree of agglutination produced: None
   (non-flocculant); Slight; Moderate; or Heavy. This
   characteristic should remain constant.

Dead-Cell Analysis

The dead-cell analysis described below uses methylene
blue solution containing sodium acetate as an
antiflocculant. Good rules of thumb for a dead-cell count
in brewer's yeast are: 5 percent is optimum, 10 percent
is good, 15 percent fair, and anything over 20 percent
should be avoided. The way to avoid a higher dead-cell
count is to use yeast as regularly as possible, and
between fermentations to keep it as cold as possible.

Methylene Blue Solution

> 0.01 g Methylene Blue
> 2.0 g Sodium Acetate (Anti-flocculant)
> 100.0 ml Distilled Water

1. Place a drop of methylene blue on a glass slide.
2. Disperse a barely visible film of yeast from the end
   of a sterile inoculating needle onto the drop of
   methylene blue.
3. Cover with a cover slip.
4. Count the percent of blue-stained cells.

This test is most accurate for low percentages of dead

cells.

Proper pitch rates are also essential. One rule of thumb is to pitch 1 million yeast cells for every degree of Plato or extract. To ferment a 12 Plato wort, you should pitch between 12 and 15 million yeast cells per ml of wort. For worts over 15 Plato, 15 to 20 million yeast cells should be pitched.

Below is a procedure for determining pitching rates to help establish an optimum number. Too few cells pitched results in longer, less-than-optimum fermentation rates. Overpitching yeast cells, on the other hand, does not allow for enough new cell growth, which may result in higher dead-cell counts.

During the course of normal fermentation, you can expect to find a maximum of approximately 60 million cells per ml of wort during the stationary phase of fermentation. This peak of 60 million cells is usually reached forty-eight hours after fermentation starts.

Determination of Pitching Rate

1. With a capillary pipet, place a drop of freshly pitched wort on each side of Neubauer hemocytometer counting chambers between the slide and cover slip. Do not let the wort extend into the moats.
2. Count the yeast cells, including those half inside the double lines, in the four corners, and in the center square of the 25- squared chamber.
3. Results:
   25 Squares = 1:10,000 ml
   5 Squares = 5 x 10,000 x number of cells = yeast cells per ml

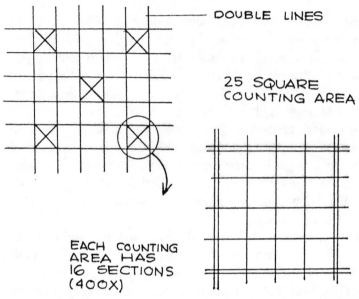

DOUBLE LINES

25 SQUARE
COUNTING AREA

EACH COUNTING
AREA HAS
16 SECTIONS
(400X)

4. If too few cells, count all 25 squares, and multiply 10,000 times the number of yeast cells per ml.

5. If too many cells, dilute the sample and include the dilution in the calculations.

If at some time during production you have less yeast than you need, you can use less wort to start with and then double up or add more wort in twenty-four hours. Doubling procedures are very effective, and can be used at any time necessary. When starting a new culture, keep doubling the amount of wort you add to the fermenter every twenty-four hours until you reach the desired volume, then let the beer ferment out. Yeast recovery should be good, as well as the beer.

Oxygen at the start of fermentation is as vital as yeast and fermentable carbohydrates. Worts should be aerated to saturation prior to and during pitching. The cooler the wort temperature at pitching, the more air it will absorb. Approximately 8 to 10 ppm dissolved oxygen is maximum. The yeast uses this oxygen during the lag phase for lipid synthesis prior to new cell development. Without wort aeration, fermentation stops prior to completion. The yeast is also weakened.

Aerating during the course of fermentation for a long time will change the yeast's metabolic pattern. Instead of producing carbon dioxide and alcohol, it will produce carbon dioxide and water. This change is known as the Pasteur effect. This will increase yeast growth, at the expense of producing beer.

The amount of carbon dioxide dissolved in beer during fermentation also affects the fermentation rate. The higher the pressure, the slower the fermentation. Large breweries use very little back pressure on fermenters -- just enough water in a water seal so that the carbon dioxide given off during fermentation can be collected for processing, cleaning, and reuse in the beer.

Optimum wort pH ranges from 5.2 to 5.4. Extremes in wort pH can affect yeast metabolism, resulting in high diacetyl levels. High beer pHs can be a problem, because the low pH of beer is one preservative factor that helps keep the beer biologically stable. It also affects final beer flavor: too acid can be too tart.

Original extract, the amount of dissolved fermentables in the wort, also affects fermentation. The more extract in the wort, the longer fermentation takes. Extracts of 15 to 19 percent may require six or seven days of fermentation instead of three to five days. This is normal, but strong worts can cause problems with a cell's water activity (the measure of the osmotic forces affecting cellular compounds). Recent research on worts with a

Plato of 35 showed that they required extra nutrition and aeration in order to ferment completely. The resulting beer was not normal.

Wort is a very good growth medium. It contains proteins, amino acids, and the vitamins and minerals necessary for fermentation. However, zinc is deficient in most worts. It is tied up or chelated by the grain and very little goes into solution. For this reason, some brewers add a trace amount of zinc to their worts to help maintain normal fermentation rates.

The conversion of acetaldehyde into ethanol and carbon dioxide is catalyzed by the enzyme alcohol dehydrogenase, and this enzyme requires zinc. A zinc deficiency limits alcohol dehydrogenase activity and slows the rate of fermentation.

The amount of zinc necessary to maintain a normal, vigorous fermentation is very small. Approximately one gram of monohydrate zinc sulfate in fifty barrels of wort is sufficient.

Temperature also affects the rate of fermentation. Cool lager fermentations take longer than 70-degree-F ale fermentations. The temperature of fermentation also affects the byproducts of yeast. Higher fermentation temperatures result in a more estery beer with lower diacetyl levels. Higher fermentation temperatures also result in higher dead cell counts.

The shape and size of the fermenter also affects fermentation. Fermenters should be built to match brew size, or multiples of your brew size plus adequate head space. You need to avoid putting a ten-barrel brew in an eight-barrel fermenter, which means you have to put two barrels somewhere else.

Long or tall, narrow fermenters may result in layering

and irregular fermentations. Conical tanks with tapered bottoms and height ratios of one to one-and-one half are ideal.

Fermenters should also be closed at the top. This helps maintain anaerobic conditions during fermentation. Of course, all the equipment being used should be easy to clean. To remove beer stone (calcium oxalate) buildup, which can harbor spoilage organisms, occasionally use a caustic solution incorporating EDTA.

Time is a fermentation goal. Yeast, aeration, nutrients, extract, filling, and emptying should be optimized to ferment the beer as fast as possible. You'll produce a better, more uniform beer and increase the capacity of your operation if you can turn your fermenters over in seven or eight days, rather than fourteen or fifteen days.

Diacetyl Production by Yeast

One of the problems faced by microbrewers and large brewers alike is the production of diacetyl by yeast. During the first two days or so of fermentation, normal yeasts produce about 0.3 or 0.4 parts per million of alpha-acetolactate. When oxidized, the acetolactate converts into diacetyl, which is detectable by taste in beer at levels less than 0.1 parts per million. Once the yeast has completed its growth phase, and under optimum conditions, the yeast metabolizes the acetolactate and reduces it to levels which, when oxidized to diacetyl, cannot be detected in the final product.

Chart C

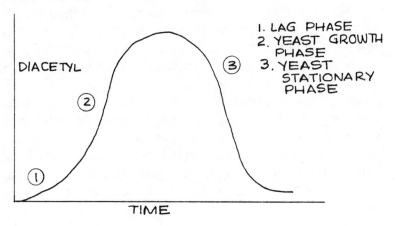

CONTROL OF DIACETYL IN FERMENTATION

1. LAG PHASE
2. YEAST GROWTH PHASE
3. YEAST STATIONARY PHASE

DIACETYL

TIME

There are three factors that are important in controlling diacetyl production in fermentation. The first is having a yeast that produces low amounts of diacetyl. As mentioned earlier, yeasts with a defective respiratory system produce greater than normal amounts of diacetyl.

Second, it is important that the wort contain adequate quantities of amino acids for good yeast nutrition. A deficiency of the amino acid valine requires the yeast to produce valine. This results in an increase in the production of the diacetyl precursor acetolactate.

Sugar --- EMP cycle --- Pyruvate --- Acetolactate --- Valine

                              Diacetyl

Finally, as mentioned earlier, it is important to maintain fermentation temperatures at the end of fermentation so the yeast can reduce and remove the acetolactate that it produced at the beginning of the fermentation cycle.

Biological Control

Of course, yeast is not the only source of diacetyl in beer, and this brings us to the discussion of the control of contaminants and organisms that can lead to off-flavors and spoilage. Once a product has spoiled, it cannot be reclaimed and should be disposed of.

Cleaning is the primary procedure for preventing spoilage -- cleaning again and again and again with hot water, steam, caustic solutions, chlorine compounds. This ensures that all surfaces that the wort or beer come in contact with do not contain residues of organisms that can initiate spoilage. When dealing with lots of equipment, however, it's often impossible to maintain "sterile" conditions. However, "commercially sterile" conditions are possible. This is where the numbers of organisms present are small enough so that they are not a threat to product spoilage.

Other than improperly cleaned equipment, yeast is the major source of most beer spoilage organisms in breweries. When you are buying yeast to start a new brewery or replacing your yeast, the only thing to do is to start with a pure culture and not with bulk yeast obtained from another brewery. once Pedicocci or Lactobacilli get into a brewery -- and their major source is bulk yeast from another brewery -- they become virtually impossible to eliminate.

Pedicocci are slow-growing anaerobic organisms that, in a brewery, grow best in the presence of yeast. Therefore, if you have a Pedicoccus problem, the easiest way to control it is by washing the yeast. Louis Pasteur proposed the first great washing procedure using tartaric acid and alcohol.

One of today's most common yeast washing procedures employs phosphoric acid. Water-diluted phosphoric acid is thoroughly mixed into the yeast, reducing the pH from 2 to 2.5 about two hours prior to pitching.

Another good method of yeast washing is with ammonium persulfate. The persulfate releases nascent oxygen that is toxic to the anaerobic bacteria, but not harmful to the yeast. The persulfate is added at a rate of of 0.75 percent by weight to the yeast. Thus 100 pounds of yeast would require .75 pounds of ammonium persulfate diluted with water. Thoroughly mix it into the yeast approximately twenty-four hours prior to pitching.

If yeast infections become particularly serious, a combination wash of phosphoric acid and ammonium persulfate can be used. Use the same quantities cited above, and add both compounds just two hours prior to pitching. Some people do not advocate yeast washing, saying that it weakens the yeast. If your yeast is in good condition, you will not notice any adverse effect. However, the best control for beer spoilage organisms is keeping them out of your brewery.

Wort is an excellent growth medium that supports the growth of all types of organisms. It contains sugar, protein, amino acids, oxygen, and has a pH of about 5.3. These conditions make it readily subject to spoilage. The common organism found in most breweries that inhabits the wort system (the area between the wort cooler and the fermenter) is Enterobacter aerogenes. If uncontrolled during fermentation, this organism produced a parsnips or spoiled, sulfury taste in the beer.

The only control for these wort bacteria are wort line sanitation and pitching a well-aerated, cooled wort with yeast as rapidly as possible. The yeast then outperforms the wort bacteria, keeping them under control. Then, as the pH drops during fermentation, these organisms die off. The fewer the bacteria, of course, the better the control.

Physically, fermented beer is completely different from wort. The pH is lower, and the fermentable sugar is gone -- as well as most of the amino acids, vitamins, and minerals. Beer is a much more stable product than wort.

During the storage of beer, two factors are vital in preventing spoilage. One is refrigeration and the other is maintaining anaerobic conditions.

Following the aging or maturation process, cold temperatures and anaerobic conditions continue to be very important. To stabilize bottled beer, it is usually pasteurized. An equivalent of 140 degrees F for ten minutes should be adequate. One minute at 140 degrees F equals one pasteurization unit (PU).

However, extremely large numbers of organisms in finished beer can result in the spoilage of pasteurized beer. Usually, the source is fermentation when uncontrolled numbers of spoilage organisms carry through into the finished beer. Maintaining biological control during fermentation is one of the most important requirements in the production of good, stable beer.

Unpasteurized bottled beer that is primed or end-fermented in the package is subject to spoilage from organisms present in the yeast. The same holds true for keg-conditioned beers where yeast is added. In Europe, brewers have had problems with the organism Zymomonas, which produces turbidity and off-flavors in draft beer.

A common problem with draft beer in this country results from having kegs in series. This usually occurs
where the lines from keg to keg or from keg to tap are
long, not kept cold, or are not properly cleaned. Once
the kegs in the series are almost empty, the keg closest
to the tap is moved to the back of the series and the new
kegs are put nearer to the tap. Now the older beer, which
previously was in the keg closest to the tap, is pushed
through the newer kegs.

If contamination with Pediococci develops in the lines
between the kegs or in the line to the draw, a strong
diacetyl flavor will develop in the beer. The only way to
correct this is to remove the contaminated kegs and line
beer out and sanitize the fittings before replacing the
beer.

As mentioned, biologically, beer is fairly stable. Hops
are bacteriostatic, meaning they inhibit the growth of
many organisms, primarily most gram positive bacteria.
The important exceptions are the lactics; Pedicocci,
which produce diacetyl; and some lactobacilli, which produce lactic acid.

Gram-negative bacteria are not as significant as the
lactics in beer spoilage, although they are hop resis-
tant. Enterobacter, the wort bacterium, usually dies off
during fermentation. Zymomonas produces hydrogen sulfide,
acetaldehyde (an apple taste), and turbidity in beer.

In 1978, the laboratories at Coors Brewery reported a
new beer-spoilage organism which they named Pectinatus.
This organism produces propionic acid and hydrogen sulfide in beer.

Acetobacter utilizes the alcohol in beer to produce
acetic acid under aerobic conditions. Other beer spoilage

organisms are Megasphaera, a coccus, and flavobacterium, which grows in long filaments.

Wild yeast, such as Saccaharomyces pastorianus, can also create problems during fermentation by producing hazes and offflavors. Mutants of your own yeast strain can produce off-flavors in your beer such as diacetyl or 4 vinyl guaiacol. Saccharomyces diastaticus ferments dextrins and produces 4 vinyl guaiacol.

To summarize biological control in the brewery, the most important factors are sanitation and good yeast management to produce clean fermentations. Keeping biological control during fermentation is of utmost importance. This is where most biological problems occur. Sanitation, keeping out air, and keeping the beer cold following fermentation are also essential.

The Future

What does the future hold? Change, undoubtedly.

There will be new genetically manipulated yeasts available that will eliminate certain problems or produce special beers.

Fermentation procedures should stay pretty much the same. We'll see a continuation of large-scale batch fermentations as we have today. Continuous fermentation has several basic problems, and I don't believe the brewing industry will go in that direction for a long time -- with the exception of calcium alginate immobilized yeast units which may eventually be used to produce a uniform beer on a small scale in microbreweries. Keg conditioning, adding yeast to the bottle, and packaging beer in bottles will probably result in the identification of new beer spoilage organisms, such as the 1978 discovery of

Pectinatus at Coors.

New breweries will be started, and big breweries will get bigger or smaller and be merged or go out of business. The same will happen to the microbreweries, and the survivors will be those that produce quality products under optimum conditions.

Mr. Van Engel is Quality Control manager at Blitz-Weinhard Brewing Company, a division of G. Heileman Brewing Company. He has over thirty years' experience in brewing-quality control and is the author of several research papers on yeast and microorganisms in brewing. He holds an M.S. in agricultural microbiology from the University of Wisconsin and is a member of the American Society for Microbiology, the Institute of Brewing, and the American Society of Brewing Chemists.

6. Marketing the Pub Brewery

Arnie Winograd

Brewing Systems Inc.
Fort Walton Beach, Florida

The brewing industry is a very cannibalistic industry at the moment. I would guess that all of the microbreweries have less than one-tenth of 1 percent of the total beer market. However, there is a large market out there, and even 1 percent represents $370 million worth of business for you to share. So from a marketing standpoint, it's a worthwhile business to pursue.

I went on the preconference microbrewery tour, which makes me an expert on small breweries and brewpubs. I believe that microbrewers are the best-educated group of people I've met. They are MBAs, schoolteachers, doctors, lawyers, brewmasters -- but only four I've met are marketing people. That's too bad, because this is not a charitable business. You are here to make a profit. You can make great beer or bad beer, but if you don't make a profit, you don't exist. And that's where marketing comes in.

The first rule of marketing is, make a marketable product. Undercapitalized hobbyists who are entering this business have a big problem. The professional investors are beginning to look at the brewing business for one reason only: because they believe it's a growth industry in which they can make an honest buck, while incidentally putting out a good beer. Without good product, you have nothing to market. That is the first marketing dictum.

Let me give you two examples of events that happened to megabreweries. (Incidentally, I make no apology for working for Pabst for twenty-six years; it gave me enough money to retire.) Schlitz Brewing Company lost its share of the market because of taste. Are you aware of that? Schlitz began a fast-brew process to make more money. In making more money, it produced a beer that was thinner and showed every inconsistency and defect in the beer -- and there are always defects in beers. As a result, the consumer didn't like the beer, and Schlitz lost out. This shows the importance of product to marketing. To successfully market, you need a great product.

For a reverse, look at Miller Lite. It is a great product, and one of the great marketing successes in American history. It isn't due to the advertising, or to an athlete; it's due to the fact that Miller came out with a product that had great consumer acceptance.

You are at a disadvantage if you don't bottle. Why? Because bottling gives you a label. Through your bottle, your graphics and name can become known and gain you public attention. If you only have kegs, what is your identification? You have a tap handle.

Microbrewers and pubbrewers have the biggest egos in the world. I never met a bunch of people with more ego. Do you know why I say that? Because you all think you brew the best product.

My point is that you all believe you're making a great product, and that's fine. But there's an old adage in the dogfood business: do the dogs like it? This applies to the beer business. Do the consumers like your beer? If you find that you sold 3,000 barrels of beer, and sales suddenly drop to 2,000 barrels, worry about your product -- no matter how good you personally think it is.

On another issue, no one here, with a few possible exceptions, has the money to really market his beers. Yet you can market your product. Take Spinnaker's Brewpub for example. Spinnaker's has eleven beers. It features a beer-ofthe-month, as new beers are introduced and old beers are retired. This is a very good marketing tool that keeps people coming in. It's a consistent way of offering enticement to try a new product.

As an aside, Spinnaker's food costs are 40 percent, compared with 32 percent nationwide. Yet the owners put more money into their foods to accompany their good beers.

Conversely, Island Pacific essentially has one, main, very good beer, not eleven. Although Island Pacific has a secondary brand, the brewery doesn't sell as much of it. But Island Pacific produces 10,000 barrels of its one lager beer, and that's without bottling. How did they capture that market?

The law in that area changed. Restaurants could not previously serve beer, but when the law changed, Island Pacific began producing draft beer in a Sankey keg. I'm not promoting Sankey, but it is an easy keg to use and to clean. Essentially, the Sankey keg became a marketing device for Island Pacific, and now most of the area uses Sankey.

Island Pacific also had a good relationship with distributors. Island Pacific understood the relationship between a brewery and its distributor.

From a marketing standpoint, there are four distributors in every market in the United States: they are the Budweiser distributor, who is making money; the Coors distributor in the West; the distributor who handles Heileman and a number of other brands; and the distributor who has Stroh, Blitz-Weinhard, or Pabst and a number of other brands.

The Bud distributor may or may not give you space on the truck. The nicest thing that could happen is that Budweiser could say to you, "Guys, I can't take you because of Bud." If that were to happen to me, I'd get the best lawyer in the world and get more publicity than anyone who ever lived.

But in the real world there are fourteen beers on the truck and twenty-two packages. Why should anyone sell your beer? You cannot afford advertising. One brewer here got trapped into neon tap handles, which cost from $100 to $200 each. And once you give point-of-sale to one customer, you have to supply it to others. So, as best you can, stay away from point-of-sale, although the bars will encourage your to spend your money on it.

Your best marketing device, in my opinion, is you. You should make yourself the hero. Let's talk about American industry for a second. Who knows who Bill Coors is? Everyone does. Who knows who Peter Stroh is? Everyone does. Who knows who Augie Busch is? Everyone does. Who knows who is president of General Motors? It's not Lee Iacocca, although he is the first person who recently brought personality to the auto business.

The point is, no one knows who is president of GM. But in beer, there is always an identity. I know Buffalo Bill Owens (Buffalo Bill's Brewpub, Hayward, California), and I live in Portland, Oregon. For some reason, the press likes to pick up on stories about beer. You have a very vital industry, and you, yourself, are vital to the industry.

Let me give you some advice. If you stand in the back of the brewery stepping on cockroaches and swatting fruit flies, you're out of your mind. Certainly you should worry about the brewing process, and I'm not downplaying that. On the tour, everyone asked about the alpha value of hops. I don't even know what that means, although everyone else seems to. But they don't know what a barrel of beer sells for on the market. Have they written a business plan, a marketing plan? Have they looked three years hence? Do they know what their cash supply is? These issues too are the business of brewing.

In the big breweries of the United States the president and CEO -- which is what you are at your brewery -- get paid $200,000 to $500,000 a year. I hope you're all making that. On the $200,000 scale, the next best-paid person is the vice-president of sales. Then there's the vice-president of marketing. I was a senior vice-president of marketing, and the sales guy always made $20,000 more than I did.

On that same scale, somewhere down at the $50,000 level, is the vice-president of production. That's true of any food product sold in the United States, and you sell a food product. The head of marketing at Coca Cola makes $700,000 a year, including his total compensation package. I'm sure the guy in charge of production at Coke doesn't make anywhere near that.

The point is, you have to be visible. If you have a little production help and therefore have the time, make some sales calls. I'd wager that 50 percent of microbrewers don't make sales calls, after a few initial calls to get the feel of the market. Know your customer.

You can be his hero.

I may be talking to a potential Augie Busch. Will he please stand up? No one is standing.

At the time Prohibition began, there were from 1,000 to 3,000 breweries in the U.S. So the microbrewing business isn't exactly new. Of those, 600 came back in 1933, and those that succeeded did so because of their marketing prowess. The failure of Pabst was in part, a marketing failure. Not seeing the trend, not bringing out a light beer fast enough, not getting that share of light-beer market was Pabst's downfall.

In marketing yourself, go out there, and tell people about your beer. It's the cheapest and best form of advertising. Take the state of Illinois, for example. It's a large state with a high per capita consumption and with microbreweries just coming in. Think what would happen if you were the first brewer there who made noise. You'd be in the New York Times.

I repeat, your best marketing asset is yourself. When you go home from this conference, go to the mirror and kiss it. There's your total resource. Realistically, I'm saying that a good product is important, but you are your most important tool.

Another important key is, put your marketing plan in writing. It's the mental exercise of trying to find out where you are going. It's a detailed analysis of every little aspect of your marketing plan. For example, what does your beer actually cost you versus its sales price? On the preconference trip, not once did any of the tour-goers ask what the beer was selling for to the distributor, to the retailer. At the brewpub, it's easy to figure: if you don't have an 800-percent mark-up, get out of business. But when you're selling through a distributor, it's another issue.

I hope you all took a financial and marketing course. I hope you know that if you're going from producing 3,000 barrels to 7,000 barrels in three years, you're going to have to start advertising. You'll have to insert the cost of advertising. You know you'll have to have the capital to put on a new machine, but do you know you'll have to insert the cost of advertising?

Financial plans and marketing plans are extremely important in these days of growing competition. I'd wager that within the next two years there will be another hundred breweries or brewpubs open. Why? Because it doesn't take much capital, when you think about it. On the tour, we looked at many homemade breweries that were not capital intensive. It's when you grow that you become capital intensive.

I can't give you any secrets of marketing, other than to remind you to watch out for the trap of point-of-sale. And to look for good design of your image. I cannot tell you to do what the big breweries do, because you'd use your budget in three minutes. You can't afford $1,000 worth of signs in an outlet. Virginia is the greatest state in the union because its law prohibits point-of-sale in taverns. If you have any influence in your state, get that law passed, and you'll be on an even basis with the big breweries.

You must look for a marketing device that is correct for your marketplace, your budget, and your image. I give a special kudos to brewpubs where food is served. If you're allowed to serve food, liquor, and novelties, you have one hell-of-a profit center. You're not depending on any one thing. And maybe you can have a 1,000 percent markup.

Distributors may work on only a 20 to 40 percent markup. Do you know what the big breweries work on? The old rule of thumb was 18 percent. Some products were marked up less than 18 percent, some more, but that was the general rule to reach the profit profile. If it wasn't met, the brewery went out of business.

Don't, by all means, put a suggested retail price on your product. If you do, you're nuts. Why ask for $1 when you could get $2? Don't undervalue your product. Price it correctly. Be arrogant about it. You're making the best product in the history of brewing. Even the ancient Egyptians didn't make better product than you do. Price in America certainly denotes quality.

I leave you with that positive thought.

Arnie Winograd is the executive vice-president of marketing at Brewing Systems Inc. in Fort Walton Beach, Florida, where he provides complete consulting services to the microbrewing industry. He has thirty-five years' experience in the brewing industry, including twenty-six years with Pabst Brewing Company as a senior vice-president.

7. Community of Brewers

Charles Baker

President, American Society of Brewing Chemists
Detroit, Michigan

On behalf of the American Society of Brewing Chemists, I want to extend our greetings and best wishes for a successful, productive, and informative conference. I thank Mr. Charlie Papazian for the opportunity to publicize and promote the services and benefits available from the ASBC. Since the technical expertise of ASBC is multidisciplinary, I welcome this occasion to exchange ideas and discuss the challenges and issues of mutual interest and importance to our industry.

First, a few words about ASBC. ASBC was founded in 1934, and was established to conduct, promote, and encourage scientific research in brewing and related industries; to study, develop, and adopt uniform methods for the analysis of raw materials, supplies, and products for and of the brewing, malting, and related industries; to hold meetings and disseminate technical knowledge; and to maintain high professional standards. Worldwide membership affirms the commitment of ASBC to achieving these goals of excellence.

ASBC offers a number of scientific services. Five service programs are available for monitoring laboratory accuracy and precision and are offered to both members and nonmembers. A statistical summary of resultant data is provided to each check service subscriber. These internal laboratory checks are available for malt, beer, hops, cereal adjuncts, and syrup adjuncts. Another service is the availability of standardized malt for the calibration of laboratory analysis.

Other ASBC services include the study of soluble starch used for the determination of malt diastatic power. Before distribution, each slide is verified for its ability to give the same analytical results. Barley and malt screens are purchased by ASBC in lots which allow single sets to be sold at minimum prices.

Society publications include the Journal of the American Society of Brewing Chemists and the ASBC Newsletter, each of which is distributed on a quarterly basis. The Journal provides a forum for the refereed publication of original research, findings and/or new applications, symposium topics, and review articles. The Newsletter is the vehicle through which current administrative, local-section, and committee activities are provided to ASBC members and subscribing nonmembers.

In addition to these quarterly publications, the ASBC publishes its Methods of Analysis. This authoritative volume of official laboratory methods is the cornerstone of ASBC. It is periodically revised and updated to maximize accuracy and precision. The technical and statistical validity of the approved ASBC methods is reinforced by publication in AOAC Official Methods of Analysis, without further collaborative study.

The overall viability and effectiveness of any formal structured organization are determined by the strength and commitment of its local support. This is not differ-

ent for the ASBC. A major contributor to the current recognition and strength of ASBC has been and will continue
to be the active growth and professional development of
local sections. As so aptly stated by a previous ASBC
president, "Local sections are a very important part of
heightened Society activities and are vital to our cont-
inuing existence and growth."

Active, local-section participation is the energy that
fuels the effective technical and social programs of
ASBC. The ASBC is stronger now than at any time in its
past fifty-two years. ASBC strength is built on the
foundation of past accomplishments, such as the
resolution of the nitrocity and biogenic amine
controversies. Society members and leadership are not
resting on the laurels of past achievements, but are
active participants in the rapidly changing technology of
today and the future.

This diversified base of ASBC technical expertise becomes more critical during these times of consolidating
and changing industry membership, as the professionalism
of ASBC has been, is, and will be derived from managing
not only the changing technology, but also the process of
change. No matter how analytically or technologically sophisticated ASBC has been or will become, it views the
future as an opportunity to excel. Part of this future
excellence is a commitment to expand the perception of
the ASBC within the brewing and allied industries from
the society to our Society. Establishing mutually benefi-
cial communications between you, the microbrewer, and the
ASBC will advance the scientific and technological requirements facing our industry.

Let me tell a little story here. Things are never
status quo. I know that as a company, Stroh is totally

supportive of the microbrewers because they provide a product and service that reaches a market the larger breweries cannot reach because of the economies of scale. Things cannot be done today like they were a few years ago -- which reminds me of the pig-in-a-wheelbarrow example.

A farmer had a sow that he wanted to have bred. The farmer next door had the proper equipment, so the first farmer loaded his sow in a wheelbarrow, and took her next door. After a couple of hours, he put the sow back in the wheelbarrow and took her home.

Well, he did this for some time, and couldn't understand why his sow didn't become pregnant. Every morning, he'd load her in the wheelbarrow and take her next door, to no avail. He asked his neighbor what he thought the trouble was. But he didn't have the answer, so the farmer with the sow decided to keep trying.

Several weeks later, the sow still wasn't pregnant. Then the farmer looked outside one morning, and there she was, lying in the wheelbarrow waiting for him to come out and wheel her next door.

The moral of this story is you have to take responsibility for the way things are today, adapt to changes, and listen to input from industry members. Business cannot be conducted today as it was in the past.

You as microbrewers have definite input to give to a brewing society, especially one like the ASBC that is based on technology and scientific research designed to meet all industry requirements. It is important that you voice your opinion and become members of the ASBC. The best place to start is with local sections and build up from there.

Charles Baker is president of the American Society of Brewing Chemists. He received a Ph.D. in biochemistry from Purdue University. He supervised evaluative research on North Dakota barley and worked as manager of brewing R&D for Pabst Brewing Company, then as manager of the Technical Center for Joseph Schlitz Brewing Company. He became director of the Technical Center with the merger of the Stroh Brewing Company and Schlitz.

8. Montana Beverage's Kessler Brewery

Daniel J. Carey

Brewmaster
Helena, Montana

Kessler Brewing Company was originally founded in 1865. Then, nearly a century later, it went out of business in the mid-1950s, along with many other regional breweries. But with its long, long history, the Kessler name is still well remembered in Helena and throughout Montana. With that in mind, Bruce DeRosier and Dick Bourke decided to revive the old Kessler label in 1978 and produce specialty beers to be sold only in Montana.

Their idea resulted in the present operation known an Montana Beverages Ltd., which was formed in 1982 as a subchapter S corporation. The initial investment was $300,000. I was hired in 1982 to perform three tasks for DeRosier and Bourke. First, I was to design their brewery on an equipment budget of $100,000. Second, I was to oversee its construction. Third, I was to become its brewmaster. At that time, I was twenty-two years old and a recent graduate of the Malting and Science program at the University of California -- Davis.

I completed all of these tasks, and we now produce the three original Kessler beers -- Kessler, Lorelei, and Kessler Bock -- and three other ultrapremium beers.

The brewery itself is situated in a warehouse owned by the corporation. The bulk of the warehouse is rented to our local distributor for storage, and the brewery comprises an area of 10,000 feet.

As I mentioned, we produce six beers, all based on my design. Two are sold year-round and four are seasonal. Our two flagship beers are Kessler, a full-bodied, pale lager, and Lorelei Extra Pale, a voll-bier that is full-flavored but less satiating.

One of our seasonal beers is Kessler Bock, a traditional 19- degree-Plato beer that Michael Jackson said is the best bock in America. We produce that in the spring. In the summer we produce a Bavarian Weizen beer brewed with Saccharomyces delbruckii and finished with S. carlsbergensis in the traditional manner. In the fall, we produce an Oktoberfest, and in the winter, a Holiday beer, which is a fruity, dry-hopped lager. Each beer is an all-malt and adheres to the Purity Law.

We do not formally advertise. Rather, we rely on what I call advertising by nonadvertising. For example, during our first year of production, we received valuable free coverage from local newspapers and television stations. We also have developed large posters that read "Montana's Own World Class Beer Available Here."

For retail outlets we also provide table tents, shelf talkers, and six-pack inserts. We gain a great deal of local recognition by sponsoring softball teams and racquetball tournaments. However, I feel that our most valuable advertising is word-of-mouth.

The brewery itself is a 3,000-barrel per annum lager plant based on a 30-barrel-capacity brewhall. The beer is both bottled and kegged. In 1985, which was our first full year of production, we sold 1,600 barrels in Montana. We outsold all imports, including Heineken. This year we have expanded our market into Spokane.

Because I deal strictly with production, I'd like to tell you about that. A microbrewer needs to be versatile. He needs a sound understanding of not only the science of brewing but also of more practical disciplines such as welding and equipment maintenance. For example, I do most of the mechanical work at Montana Beverages, including heliarc welding.

Then I use skills different from those needed in welding when I work in the laboratory. We maintain a small but adequate lab to perform the necessary quality control and assurance. The list of lab equipment we have is as follows:

1. Temperature-corrected hydrometers
2. Hand-held refractometer
3. pH meter and pH paper (0-13)
4. Thermometers
5. .02 N Iodine
6. Water hardness and calim tester
7. Brightfield microscope and various plate media
8. CO_2 volume meter
9. Zahm Nagel air tester and S.S. bottle for bulk beer air testing
10. A balance
11. Various glassware

Our water source for both cleaning and brewing is a seventymeter-deep well. A well is nice because it gives a relatively consistent water composition and is less expensive than city water.

I constructed the mash tun from a dairy bulk-storage tank. It contains an agitator and false bottom purchased from a major western brewery. We purchase all our malt in sacks. It is milled through a two-roll Roskamp mill into a steel hopper on skids. It takes about thirty minutes to mill 1,500 pounds of malt.

We do not have any automatic grain handling, and all of our grain handling is done with an electric forklift. The grist hopper is carried from the milling room to the mash tun, and poured into the top as the agitator turns. I use either a single-temperature infusion or a two-step infusion process, depending on the beer. In the case of the step infusion, I first start with a very thick protein rest and add boiling water to achieve saccharification. Sparge water comes directly from the hot-water machine. With this design, I get close to 70 percent extract.

Mashing and lautering are performed in the same tank. The wort is gravity fed into a grant/surge tank through a flow meter. From there it is pumped into the kettle whirlpool, which is natural-gas fired. It achieves an excellent rolling boil and clean hot break. Whirlpooling is performed in the same tank.

The hopped wort is then pumped through a two-stage plate heat exchanger. The first stage, cooling, is with city water and the second with chilled ice water. The ice water is produced in an Ice Building Machine, which consists of a five-ton freon compressor coupled to an insulated water tank. It takes one hour to cool thirty barrels of wort from 210 to 50 degrees F.

After cooling, the wort is pumped into the cellars. I use a unitank system because of the advantages offered to the microbrewer. For one, it requires less capital expenditure because both fermentation and lagering occur in the same tank. It requires less labor because there is no transfer from fermentation to lagering and only half as many tanks to clean. Also, since there is no transfer, there is less chance of picking up air or microbial organisms.

The cone bottoms make yeast repitching simple. Settled yeast can easily be transferred through a sterile hose to the next batch. Also, the cone bottom makes removal of dead yeast and cold break simple and clean.

The fermentation temperatures vary depending on the particular beer. For example, Lorelei Extra Pale is fermented at 46 degrees F for ten days, while primary for the Weizen is 60 degrees F for four days. Lagering lasts five to ten weeks at 32 degrees F.

Each of our unitanks is sixty-five barrel capacity and can hold one week's production, which is 2, thirty-barrel brews. I designed them and had them built in Boise, Idaho.

After lagering, the beer is processed through a pressure-leaf filter using kieselguhr and a small amount of silica gel. We have a Velo unit that can run sixty-barrel batches in one hour. Because we use only a single-pass filtration, this operation must be flawless. The finished beer is quite brilliant by industrial standards.

The filtered beer is transferred into a brite beer tank where it is stored until bottling or kegging. A pump is not employed to move the beer to the filler. Rather, a carbondioxide head pressure is utilized to push the beer to the filler bowl. This method results in less agitation of the beer than pumping.

The bulk of the beer is sold in twelve-ounce bottles. The bottle shop consists of a Cem 28-6 Uniblend filler and a World Tandem Labeler. It operates at between seventy and eighty bottles per minute, and averages 1.5

ml of oxygen per twelve-ounce bottle (as low as 0.5 ml). Short fill average is about one percent. The secret to a low short-fill rate is good consistent filler maintenance.

Daniel Carey resigned his position at Montana Beverages Ltd. as of September 1986, and will work in Europe during 1987 at three renowned traditional breweries in England and Germany.

9. The Good News Is You're Getting Larger

R. Corbin Houchins

Attorney at Law
Seattle, Washington

For most of us, an upward sales curve looks like an unqualified blessing -- and all other things being equal, it is.

The problem, of course, is that all other things in a growth phase are never equal. Operating costs and capital requirements are up; available managerial time and energy are down. The result is a good-news/bad-news picture that requires some planning if you are going to make the good predominate.

Starting Now

As any parent can tell you, the best time to plan for growth is before it occurs. Unfortunately, conventional wisdom on timing is difficult to apply in practice. Before you open your doors, you probably don't have enough information to set target sales volume and calculate the cash needs to get there. By the time you do have that information, you are probably devoting every waking hour to survival -- so a growth-management plan gets put off again.

Last-Minute Shopping List

Most growth planning occurs only when someone begins to feel the growing pains. If you are planning ahead, that's great. But planning is still timely if you are already growing and have begun to get the feeling that procedures and plans now in place are no longer adequate.

I should say at the outset that no one can tell you how to make a growth plan without knowing the specifics of your business and the people in it. Furthermore, you certainly ought to include your banker, accountant, and lawyer in the process. Thus, you are not going to leave here with a recipe for managing growth. You will, I hope, take from this session some points to cover in the course of working out a growth plan.

So let's start a checklist.

Some Steps to a Growth-Management Plan

1. Assess methods of increasing managerial resources.
2. Anticipate problems in personnel management.
3. Investigate sources of capital.
4. Put legal framework for raising capital in place before beginning implementation.
5. Ascertain changes in business structure required by new people and capital.
6. Evaluate noncapitalized alternatives.
7. Analyze space and location needs.
8. Evaluate insurance alternatives.
9. Define present and fully grown businesses.
10. Determine optimum size.

Managerial Resources

The first item is managerial resources. A larger enterprise needs more management, and hence, "Assess methods of increasing managerial resources."

When most brewery founders approach the need to increase managerial resources, they think of personnel expansion. Typically, existing managers hire someone to do tasks that require less judgment, so they have time for higher-level decisions. That may or may not be a good course of action, depending on the strengths of the founders. Sometimes the best course is to keep the original team doing what it was doing and hire a controller or other new team member.

The first item on the laundry list does not read "hire subordinates," but says in effect, "Look at all alternative ways to increase managerial resources."

If you hire people, new legal issues arise regarding terms of employment. Some of you may have seen the issue of *The New Brewer* that contained a discussion on hiring brewmasters. In the case of a production person, it is usually (but not always) fairly straightforward to spell out what the person is to do. But that does not apply across the board, which brings us to item number two on the list: "Anticipate problems in personnel management."

In a growth situation, where management is facing unfamiliar challenges, it is all too easy to skip the step of thinking through exactly what the duties of a new employee will be and how much authority that employee will have.

New sales and financial positions are notorious for being inadequately defined.

Sales People

Too often, managers who are production oriented believe that the job of sales is to cause however many barrels are put on the dock to be converted into money, without having any impact on what goes on inside the brewery.

In real-world sales, growth can be sustained only by responding to the challenges and opportunities of the market. Being responsible for sales means being the eyes and ears of the brewery in the marketplace, and devising plans based on what is seen and heard. That involves pricing; timing and volume of production; and, of course, the kind of products that must be offered in order to achieve the sales increases desired by management. Where the buck stops on those issues, and whether and to what extent the salesperson's recommendations are to be implemented, are just two sensitive items that must be negotiated as part of any employment understanding with a new salesperson.

Financial Consultants

Confusion about what financial people are hired for is also common. Few managers would admit that they hired an accountant or bookkeeper for the purpose of making the numbers agreeable, or to keep from having to think about the numbers -- but in practice, those expectations creep in.

Growth almost always presents a fair number of very disagreeable facts -- facts from which high-quality decisions must be made if the business is to survive. Adding financial specialization to your management resources, either by hire or by retaining an accounting firm, can get the facts to you more promptly and accurately, accompanied by useful analysis and a statement of options with probable results. It doesn't, however, take financial considerations off the manager's plate.

Personnel Management

Another skill whose importance becomes more noticeable in a growth phase is personnel management. Managing the relations among people is a separate task with its own requirements. Some of them are just a matter of having a sufficiently specialized base of experience to work from in a tricky area. Part of the job is compliance with laws regulating industrial relations. Especially as you increase in size and begin to trade across state lines, you find yourself subject to additional legal requirements.

People who start businesses generally handle personnel matters with whatever skills and traits they happen to possess. But a growing business needs personnel-management skills of a high order, if it is to avert people problems. Long before you reach the size where a specialist should be hired, someone has to wear the personnel-manager hat, and he or she should be given the authority (and if need be, the training) to handle it well.

Although we put a personnel-management plan as point two in dealing with growth, there is, in fact, no ranking in this list -- and, with a couple of exceptions, no chronological order of the considerations. All the items need attention at the outset, although their relative urgency and the sequence of dealing with them varies from business to business.

Capital Needs

This brings us to another topic that is clearly of primary importance: capital, which is number three on the list -- "Investigate sources of capital."

Regardless of our politics, when we are in business, we are capitalists. Every business, including nonprofit and charitable trust, has to have a capital budget (whether or not we recognize it as such), and has to be aware of sources of capital.

For the purposes of this discussion, I will adopt a very unscientific definition of the new capital needs of a growing company. Capital is what you need to get your checkbook back up to zero after you've deposited all your income and written checks to cover all your payables, plus put a bit aside for future expenses.

Now, that doesn't sound like a rosy picture. You might ask, "If I'm growing, why do I need more money just to stay at zero?" The answer is going to sound like Murphy's Law. It is simply that the costs of growth nearly always arrive before the revenues. Hence, the need for planning for growth.

Of course, you can't know what your capital needs are until you know how much you are going to grow, and no one has a crystal ball for future sales. It is a relatively simple process, however, for your accountant or friendly banker to project cash needs versus revenues at several assumed higher sales levels. The major complication is that you really have to keep going back to it as your plan is affected by other considerations, some of which we'll cover later on the checklist.

Chances are that any realistic growth scenario is going to require additional capitalization to bridge the gap between higher expenses and actual receipt of income. This brings up a key item in your growth plan: where and how will you obtain the new capital you need?

Internal Sources

You should first get together with your accountant and look for sources of capital within the business. This may be a good time to consider accounts-receivable policies, collection methods, and other ways of improving cash flow. It may also be appropriate to determine how much of your earnings should be committed to reserves for one thing or another, and how much, if any, there is of retained earnings to finance growth.

It will be a rare microbrewery indeed that discovers underutilized, retained earnings that are sufficient to meet a growth plan. Nevertheless, don't skip the step of looking. You don't want to borrow more than you have to, but you do want to allocate to your growth plan whatever you need to reach your optimum size.

Lenders

This brings us to outside sources of new capital. Obtaining new capital from outside sources is one area where accountants and lawyers can wax creative, if not poetic. The variations on the theme of acquiring the use of other people's money are infinite, and I will not attempt to describe them here.

For the purposes of our discussion, let's stick to the basics: Essentially, you will need to borrow more (cash from banks, trade credit from suppliers); apply retained earnings; make further equity investments; or (and this is often the soundest course) both borrow and invest. Let's look at sources of borrowed funds.

Bankers. I hope your banker likes both your beer and your balance sheet, because he or she is probably going to have to participate with you in weakening the balance sheet -- at least for an interval -- in order to make way for more beer.

Weakening a balance sheet sounds like a terrible thing to do -- and indeed, it is serious business that should be undertaken only for a reasonable expectation of gain. By borrowing to finance growth, you will, at least in the near term, make your solvency and liquidity ratios look scarier than they already are. This is because the debt entry is going to get bigger before cash and accounts receivable reflect the presumed higher level of sales.

In the course of that frightening procedure, you will (if you are successful in obtaining loans) be presented by your proposed lender with several pages of forms. About two sides of one sheet will be statements you make to the banker about your financial condition and that of your business. There will be a form confirming that you have been told certain things about the interest rate. About two lines at the top of one page will constitute a promise to pay the money back, with interest. There may also be a stipulation restricting your right to incur other debts while this lender is unpaid.

All the rest of the pages of compact type come under the heading of "or else." In other words, they say what happens if you don't pay on time -- and they will probably rely on that sincerest of promises, the secured negotiable note.

Careful analysis of needs and capacity, consideration of alternatives, and thorough legal review are called for before you sign. Thus, this is going to take some time.

Trade creditors. The second source of borrowing is less straightforward, as it involves lenders who in many cases do not like to admit they are in the business of lending: your trade creditors, broadly defined.

If you have been in business for a while with a good record of paying your bills on time, and can show a growth trend (or at least a sensible plan to become a bigger customer). you are in a good position to have a heart-to-heart talk with the people behind that stack of bills in the payables tray.

The subject will be better terms of payment. The positive side you wish to present is that you are a good, reliable account, and it would be in your supplier's best interests to keep you -- even at the cost of temporarily inferior cash flow as the volume increases. Your objective, of course, is to convince him to allow you to pay at longer intervals.

For example: you may ask that you be allowed to pay net thirty or ninety days the same as cash, with the supplier eating the higher cost to him, in hopes that you will be a higher-volume account in the future.

Note that there may be some restrictions on the level of accounts payable you may maintain consistently while you have a loan agreement with a bank, so the two kinds of borrowing must be coordinated. Also, if your borrowing from one creditor is secured, the security is not going to be available to another creditor. Therefore, you can't give a trade supplier a security interest in anything you expect to pledge to the bank. Generally, the bank gets security, the supplier gets hopes.

Suppliers. I haven't discussed borrowing from your suppliers by simply paying more slowly without any prior agreement. That is a tricky area from the standpoint of legal ramifications, as well as business ethics. Moreover, if you are serious about growing, a reputation for timely payment will be worth far more to you than the interest charges on the money you might have to borrow to avoid shorting your trade accounts.

Equity Structure

To borrow funds, you have to promise to repay, regardless of how profitable or unprofitable your business is.

To obtain funds without promising to repay, you generally have to give away a piece of the action. How much, and on what conditions, you share ownership in your business depend largely upon your salesmanship and your lawyer's imagination -- both of which are, I hope limitless. We can, however, sketch out a few general considerations. This is number four on the list, "Put legal framework for raising capital in place before beginning implementation."

Investing more of your own money in a sole proprietorship is largely a personal and accounting matter. Investing other people's money adds serious legal issues and requires great care.

This item on the checklist is going to vary according to the nature of your business, but it's probably going to raise the following issues:

1. Compliance with local and federal law regarding how many and what kind of people you can talk to about investing; where they may be located; what documents you may and may not show them; etc.;

2. What voice in management you are willing to grant

in order to get funds;

3. Contingency plans for new investors coming in, old investors going out, and all investors falling out with one another.

Organizational Structure

As an organization becomes larger, a high degree of organization is required. Hence the fifth adage: "Ascertain changes in business structure required by new people and capital."

The legal form of organization may need attention, so that it helps the process of distributing authority and responsibility. Formal changes must certainly be considered when new people make investments. The distinction between ownership and control is fundamental, but not obvious in the context of a small, closely knit group.

Additionally, the new tax law will put the point at which incorporation becomes desirable at a different level of net income.

The managerial structure, the real organizational chart of your business, also has to be examined. We have already spoken of the importance of precision in defining the responsibility and authority of people you hire. In a growth phase, the same goes for everyone who is still there.

There may be some tough personnel decisions when your business moves from startup to takeoff. The attention to personnel management I referred to earlier is quite essential.

Organizational structure is something that business consultants like to tinker with. The use of business consultants is a topic that could absorb a long seminar;

there is a lot of snake oil out there, and a lot of valuable advice. Unfortunately, the product does not carry a label telling you which is which. You may find that college extension courses in business-related topics are a better investment than engaging the services of someone who has a Yellow Pages listing as a business consultant.

Whatever your source of advice in this area, and whether your organizational chart has two or twenty people on it, give some attention to production capacity in the planning stage.

Production Capacity

Now let's get to something more concrete: barrelage. Sales curves are graceful, flowing lines on a chart. Costs of increasing capacity tend to be incremental, like stair steps.

Thus you must calculate production capacity increases necessitated by the various probable future sales scenarios and also find ways to minimize the effects of unpleasant surprises when the scenario plays out differently than you expected.

Contract Brewing. An expanding microbrewery should consider shared production facilities and contract brewing, as well as the conventional route of investing in more tubs and tanks. Enter the sixth item on the checklist, "Evaluate noncapitalized alternatives."

In a way, contract brewing is another method of using other people's money. More particularly, it avoids increasing the fixed costs associated with capital equipment. Admittedly, the variable costs of compensating the business with the production facility may be higher than their fixed counterparts. The price of flexibility is often justified, however, when expansion calls for a basic change in the way you operate, such as getting into bottling. If your custom brewing contract is well drawn, you will get not only the use of equipment, but also the benefit of someone else's operating experience as well.

A well-drawn brewing contract will cover a lot of ground besides use of the premises and equipment and the advice of the people who own it. There are also important trade secrecy, trademark, and regulatory issues.

Expansion

A whole new range of issues arises if you are going to need more space. The hidden costs of physical expansion are notorious, but a good accountant with experience in small manufacturing operations should be able to pencil it out for you.

There will be some major crossroads, ranging from rent versus purchase, to the relative importance of costs as compared to location and appearance. To make correct choices, you have to have a firm idea of what your business is going to be at its near-term optimum size, which is often quite different from the business you thought you were going into. This is where you "Analyze space and location needs."

Whatever you decide, you will face issues related to commercial or industrial real property on which you will need both financial and legal guidance. My advice is that you approach this item without prejudice for or against making changes, and take the time required to cost it out carefully.

Risk Management and Insurance

The next point is risk management, which is a soothing term for trying to cope with threats you can't control or predict. A growth plan has to include risk management because a bigger company has more at risk. Your mainstay in managing risk is insurance, and that is a topic which is not a happy one in these times.

Presumably you already have insurance coverage for premises and industrial accident liability, product liability, and (if you serve beer) dram shop liability. Discuss the adequacy of your coverage with your financial and legal advisors, then shop around for service, rates, and coverage. "Service" in this context means not only claims payment statistics, but also whether the agent you deal with gives you good-quality advice. It won't be disinterested advice, but it can be useful, and he or she may have some good management tips on running your operation so as to minimize risk. This is item eight on the list, "Evaluate insurance alternatives."

By the way, in ensuring physical equipment and inventory, your range of choices may be narrowed somewhat by the terms of any borrowing agreement you may have with a lender. Typically, you are required to keep full value coverage on items that are pledged to secure repayment of your loans.

The right decision on this is going to depend not only on business factors like available coverage and your insurance premium budget, but also on personal considerations, like what you have to lose and the degree of risk you and any other investors can sleep with.

New Lines of Business

The next item has to do with defining what it is you know how to do that produces profits, and deciding whether you can grow by doing more of the same thing. Appropriate here is item nine, "Define present and fully grown businesses."

I often quote business writer Peter Drucker's advice to ask yourself two questions constantly: "What business am I in?" and "What business should I be in?"

Making keg beer in quantities you can sell through your own efforts in time spared from production tasks is not the same business as marketing a brand of beer. Serving beer and selling t-shirts to the public is not the same business as brewing. Selling to taverns is not the same business as selling to distributors.

In a growth phase, look for both opportunities and hazards in crossing over into businesses you have not carried on before. Especially if you enter the packaged goods business -- that is to say bottled beer -- expect a whole new set of contractual relationships, governmental regulations, and personnel management tasks, in addition to the job of producing the new product itself.

Business textbooks are littered with case histories of companies that were very good at one kind of business, changed to another kind (either without realizing it or with the assumption that they could master anything), and died. A growth plan absolutely must be based on a clear understanding of what the business is that will produce the incremental barrelage and how you will succeed in it.

Talk to people who are already dealing with distributors, field-sales reports, chain-store buyers, advertising media, promotional pricing, price points, cold-box placement, shelf position, receivables aging, and the new competing import of the week.

In doing your personal research, listen to what they say and try to get an idea of what's involved in emotional wear and tear as well as managerial requirements. Read up on the relevant topics at a good business library. Think about staffing needs and what it will feel like to depend on employees who do essential jobs that you don't know how to do. This may look like an item worth five minutes of discussion in the tasting room, but it is really a considerable project of both research and introspection, and it is indispensable.

I have referred at times to something called "optimum size." There is a sales level or range that is right for your business under current conditions, so that your profitability would be less if you were either larger or smaller. You are probably not at that point, and you are probably not above it. Do not assume that larger is better. Instead, try to figure out what your nearterm optimum size is and, equally importantly, the rate at which you should try to get there. This is the tenth, and last point, "Determine optimum size."

I believe there are two independent considerations in this area. One is approachable by arithmetic. Some people might argue that this should have been first on this checklist, but because you have to think about all these factors together before you can start a spreadsheet, I have included it here.

Basically, you and your accountant are going to test some scenarios, using break-even analysis and other tools of the trade, to determine the following:

1. What you have to do with pricing and marketing to sell at projected volumes;

2. How to maintain debt-to-worth ratios that will allow you to sustain growth, e.g., increase inventory turnover.

3. What gaps exist in the balance sheet between needed funds and available funds that require capital infusions;

4. The extent to which you can finance the additional assets required to support higher levels of business activity.

Interest rates, competitive conditions, and a number of other things you cannot know with certainty will cause the result to be a range, rather than a number, but it is a lot better than just taking a ruler and extending historical profit-and-loss figures.

That arithmetical process is, as I said, one consideration.

The other consideration is having fun.

Few of us want to work forever in the crisis mode that typifies small business startups, even if we enjoy that environment for a while. Growth plans need size objectives, not only because marketing and financial considerations imply an optimum size, but also because human beings -- even small business operators -- seem to enjoy life more if it is at least punctuated by episodes of sanity.

A conservative estimate of how many management hours at full mental capacity you can happily devote to the business over the long haul is a key variable in determining the size to aim for.

Thus, in dealing with item ten, do not forget to consider things like having babies and going fishing. After all, mostly we are in business in order to integrate meaningful work into the larger fabric of life. Thus, the last thing on my list is to put that larger consideration into your growth plan, so that when the final spreadsheet is totaled up, you will like the balance.

R. Corbin Houchins is a partner in the law firm Duryea and Houchins in Seattle, Washington. He is a writer and lecturer on business law and on the regulation of production and sale of alcoholic beverages. He publishes regularly in The New Brewer.

10. "If I Could Do It Again..."

Wolfgang Roth
Chesapeake Bay Brewing

Don Barkley
Mendocino Brewing Company

Bill Newman
William S. Newman Brewing

Wolfgang Roth (Virginia Beach, Virginia)

We are here today to talk about problems we have had and their solutions. It's not easy for any of us to admit that we've had problems, but it's best that we share our experiences so that others can avoid them.

Chesapeake Bay Brewing Company in Virginia Beach, Virginia, is a typical microbrewery, created through a hobby of Dr. James Kollar. Dr. Kollar had been a homebrewer, and wanted to take the step from small-scale homebrewing into larger-scale microbrewing. To do this, he bought mostly used equipment. There has been a lot said at this conference about the feasibility of used equipment, and I can tell you from experience that if you cannot afford to buy new equipment, then you cannot afford to buy used equipment.

For example, we ran into problems with our stainless-steel tanks. You might think that stainless steel will last forever, but it can get fine, unnoticeable cracks. At the time our tanks developed these small cracks, we did not have the proper laboratory equipment to find the problem; instead, we found out when the beer was packaged and about ten months old.

Usually you hope to sell your beer as quickly as possible, but your distributors don't always move it as quickly as you'd like. Most distributors make most of their money selling the beers of large breweries. They sell perhaps 400 cases of Budweiser a day, compared to four or five cases of your beer. Naturally, they go where they can make the easier money. Then if the distributor doesn't sell your beer quickly enough, any flavor problem is likely to show -- as ours did. But with the proper lab equipment, you can detect the problem when it arises and correct it.

This is one important point I want to make: don't sell your beer without having the lab equipment necessary to conduct quality control. Have it in place before you brew your first batch of beer. We learned that the hard way. And the problem is difficult to correct, because once your brewery is set up, it's very expensive to take out equipment and start from scratch. Usually you can only replace it piece by piece, as you can afford to.

We're all here at this conference to share information, because we're all in the same boat. The microbrewing business is getting stronger and stronger, and more and more small brewers are entering the market -- many of whom are professionals backed by money, knowledge, and experienced personnel. But only those who can produce a good, consistent beer, and have good packaging, will survive. A lot of us will fail. But if we can raise the standards of small breweries, all of us will benefit, no matter in what area of the United States.

Don Barkley (Hopland, California)

I want to start by talking about the New Albion Brewing Company, where I worked from 1978 to 1983, before I began at the Mendocino Brewing Company. The New Albion was incorporated in 1976 (becoming the first microbrewery in the United States), made its first batch of beer in 1977, and in 1983, slowly slid under the waters for a variety of reasons. I want to tell you about one of those reasons.

Jack McAuliffe founded the New Albion Brewing Company with $10,000, by building all his brewing equipment and fermenting his beer in five-gallon carboys. A year later, he began using fifty-five-gallon stainless-steel drums scavenged from a Coca Cola distributor. But even though the New Albion didn't survive, its equipment was made to last; now it's in use in the Mendocino Brewing Company. The equipment is ten years old -- the same age as the microbrewing industry.

At Mendocino Brewing, we brew ten batches a week, at about one-and-a-half barrels per batch. In 1986, we brewed about 500 batches of beer. The point is that well-conceived equipment, based on traditional brewing practices, can and will produce good beer forever. But to build a good brewing system, a person must thoroughly understand the brewing process. He can't bounce out of homebrew and into a commercial brewery and expect to be successful.

Besides Jack's creativity in making the nation's first microbrewery, he had the quality of being a fighter. Whether you're a big brewery or a small one like New Albion, you have to fight, fight, fight for sales. New

Albion eventually got tired, tired, tired, which is one reason it's gone now. It was unable to finance the expansion it needed to survive. At its maximum output, New Albion was making 120 cases of beer a week. At that rate, we were unable to raise the $750,000 it would have taken to expand. When you can't grow, you're gone.

But the professionalism that Jack put into the production facility has survived. Professionalism in brewing -- making the beer, running the business, or selling the beer -- is absolutely essential.

Now I'd like to tell you about the Mendocino Brewing Company, which began in 1983 with the New Albion equipment. Mendocino Brewing is a limited partnership that began with $125,000. To save money, we pounded every nail in our facility, put the oak floor and bar in the tavern, and built up our beer garden. For that small amount of money, we had the first brewpub to open in California since Prohibition.

Yet, had we had the money to build a fifteen-barrel plant, we'd be farther ahead than we are now. Today we brew 450 gallons of beer a week, producing four different kinds of beers. I wish we had a larger production capacity.

A couple of months ago, I lost my professional virginity, so to speak. We began to get some beer coming along the lines that tasted peculiar. When we put the beer into bottles for conditioning, it was fine; two weeks later, it was bad. We immediately stopped serving it and investigated the cause. One good thing about having a brewpub is that you catch a problem in a shorter time than in a microbrewery.

We found several things wrong. First, a couple of valves were leaking oxygen into the beer coming out of the secondary fermenters. Also, we had recently installed some new hose that gave the beer a particular character. The combination was terrible. I lost a few nights' sleep, and we lost ten days' worth of beer. We simply rolled the tanks out the back door and dropped the beer down the drain. At least that decision saved our asses. We didn't ruin our good reputation.

The last topic I'll discuss is that I'm glad to see Thomas Reap from Master Brewers Association and Charles Baker from the American Society of Brewing Chemists at this conference. They are the mouthpiece of the brewing industry -- both micro and major brewers -- to legislators. I'd like to promote the idea of joining such associations. They are invaluable to us from the production and the political standpoint.

Bill Newman (Albany, New York)

The William S. Newman Brewing Company is a brewery in transition. In 1981, we were one of the first few microbreweries in the United States. We had traveled to Britain to study with Peter Austin, and we had the concept of being a small, English-ale, local draft brewery. At that time England was going through a revival of real ales, and we took our cues from that. We were looking for a product that would be a good substitute for what we perceived as the bland mass-market, lagers available in the U.S. We wanted something outstanding -- something we could charge a higher price for and build a business on.

We got the sequence of packaging and distributing decisions backwards. Normally, when you start a brewery, you decide how you are going to distribute your product, and then match the packaging to that. We decided, for two reasons, that we'd offer a draft product. First, we didn't want to get involved in a complex bottling operation. Second, the investment in bottling equipment would probably have doubled our initial investment, and we didn't have the leverage to do that.

The situation in England, where draft consumption is about 9 percent, also reinforced our idea to make a draft-only brewery. We decided on English-style draft ale, and then decided to focus our sales in the local area. Our distribution was within a thirty-mile radius of Albany, a city of 90,000 people.

In looking for a marketing image, we decided to tie into the renaissance in Albany, where a great deal of historical renovation was occurring. In fact, however, our image became more that of the lone, fanatical brewer with a very foreign-style beer taking on the major brewers. Our ale was very full-bodied, very distinctive -- a beer you loved or hated.

Since then, we've done a lot of thinking on the way to the bank. We've restructured our loans and changed our direction. Our current thinking is that ale is really a very small part of the market. To focus on an English-style real ale is further specializing -- unnecessarily. A marketing study for our beer questioned people about their perception of English-style ale. They were specifically asked about Albany Amber Ale, our flagship brand. We found that they perceived English ale as heavier, stronger, and sometimes warmer than other beers. With those facts, we decided we were working the wrong side of the street, and should be making a lager.

Regarding packaging, it became obvious to us that the specialty-beer market is really a bottled-beer market. I

don't want to overgeneralize, however, as I don't think
that is the case in the Northwest. Specialty-beer
drinkers are that thin uppercrust. To reach them, you
need a wide distribution, which means you need a bottle.
Draft is very heavily biased toward local marketing.
Being in Albany, we didn't have a broad enough base.

In recent years, specialty beers have gained tremendous national attention. People now have variety and
choice in their beers, and the job of the microbrewer is
to get on the bandwagon for good-quality American beers.
The image we have now acquired is that of a brewer making
real beers in the U.S. We're very proud of our art and of
restoring good qualities to beer.

The sum of this is that we are now more keenly
market-oriented than we were in the beginning. Then, our
focus was more on the product and on the brewing
process. Now, we've come to realize that we have to look
at the consumer and the market.

I'd like to make a few personal observations. We
started as an English-ale keg brewer in 1981, and have
since added to our product line Albany Amber beer in bottles, which we have produced in a larger brewery. We
really have our feet in both the brewing and con-
tract-brewing worlds. As a brewer, I'm not concerned
about the contract-brewed beers. They really help extend
the public's awareness of good-quality beers. I don't
think a brewer needs the bricks and mortar of a brewery.
In fact, I would argue that there's a good case for getting a product, achieving the quality and reputation it
needs, and then building the brewery when you've reached
an optimum point.

Nor am I overly concerned about the big breweries making specialty beers. Successful microbrewers and contract

brewers gain their momentum largely on quality products backed by personal appeal. There's a localness to each of our brands that major breweries cannot attach themselves to in any significant way. I think there will be a market niche for microbrewers despite the efforts of the major brewers.

I do see some limits on the number of specialty brews that can be successful. It's a function of the three-tier system. There is a certain number of distributors who will take on a microbrewed amber product. We recently got a distributor because he had heard about us and because we fit into the beers he carries. He was looking for an amber American beer.

The big question for those planning to start a brewery, is, how do you successfully get into the business? Contract breweries and pubbreweries are the most viable, in my opinion. Microbreweries are less viable. Yet, a person who is consumer/market oriented -- looking for a profit -- has a big advantage over people who are more interested in the brewing process.

The keys to having a successful microbrewery or pub brewery are the same as they have always been: a good, distinctive, quality product (whether a lager or an ale); a well-targeted market with a good point of sale and public-relations campaign; and a lot of personal stamina to see it through.

Q: Mr. Newman, would you start out again with a small keg brewery and then go to contract brewing?
Bill Newman: It's been a tough road. As I said, we had to restructure our debt. We do have the advantage of being able to trade off of our name and reputation as bona-fide brewers. But in answer to your question, I think that is

a backwards way to approach it, because you do have to make the capital investment.

Q: Mr. Newman, how comparable is your bottled Albany beer with your draft ale?

Bill Newman: It is our goal to make a comparable product, albeit switching from an ale to a lager, that captures the malty quality of our Albany Amber Ale. To achieve that, we use the same recipe, and ship the same hops and roasted malts to the contract brewer. Of course, the lager is different, but it captures the spirit and flavor of a good-quality amber beer.

Q: Is it going to be a problem in the future to find a distributor for microbrewed beer?

Wolfgang Roth: Big breweries don't give their beer to every distributor. They have requirements for warehouse space, refrigeration, trucking, etc., that the small, local distributors can't always meet. We are selling most of our beers through small distributors who get the product out and take more care of it than the larger ones do. The larger distributors don't always need you. More and more, the wine distributors are willing to take on beer products.

Don Barkley: I have a tip for you: Don't single-source yourself with any distributor. If a distributor is unable to push your product, conceivably you could have beer several months old on the store shelves. Beer that is not pasteurized or filtered suffers greatly after sitting in a warehouse for six months.

Also, you are not selling just to the public; you are selling to the distributor. You need to have a sales force, and you need someone who is out looking after your product fulltime. It's a big part of the business to liaison between the brewery, the distributor, and the retailers.

Bill Newman: There may be a problem with the shrinking threetier system. But more than anything, you have to give a distributor good margin on your beer, you have be sure there's going to be good volume for it, and you have to give good support for your product by being there for the distributor.

Wolfgang Roth is the Brewmaster at Chesapeake Bay Brewing Company, Virginia Beach, Virginia. He holds a master's degree in brewing and malting from Schlossbrauerei Stetten in Germany.

Don Barkley is the Brewmaster at Mendocino Brewing Company in Hopland, California.

William S. Newman is the Brewmaster and owner of William S. Brewing Company, Albany, New York, which he founded with his wife Marie in 1981. He apprenticed at the Ringwood Brewery in Hampshire, England.

11. Beer Flavor in Your Brewery

Ron Siebel

Siebel Institute of Technology
Chicago, Illinois

The topic of my presentation is beer flavor, and specifically, how it is measured. I'd like to speak first on the need for tasting, and then on some preliminaries for setting up a beer-flavor profile. This information is a very good tool in controlling beer flavor.

I'll spend the bulk of my time looking at a method of flavor profiling that was introduced to the industry in the 1960s. It was the first working profile in use in this country, and is still being used by a number of breweries. We've updated it, however, and are considering a few changes to improve it further.

Finally, I'll comment briefly on the most important factor in flavor tasting: the individual taster.

There are three important factors from the standpoint of tasting, the first of which is evaluation. Evaluating beer means going beyond simply asking if it is good or bad, do you like it or not. This is when you ask which components of your beer make it different from others, and how you can regulate the intensity of natural components -- for example, the amount of hoppiness, bitter-

119

ness, maltiness, etc. -- to achieve the flavor you want.

Consistency is another factor that has caused brewers difficulty over the years. Consistency can be very elusive, but it is probably the most important factor from a consumer's standpoint. Therefore, it is necessary that you taste and profile your beer in order to detect minor changes in flavor and to monitor the consistency.

Finally, defects are important to identify so they can be isolated and corrected. For example, if you start detecting taste thresholds of diacetyl in your beer, you may wish to check your fermentation cycle and correct it before the taste becomes so manifest that it is detectable by consumers.

I'll speak briefly on the glossary of beer-flavor attributes, which gives us definitions for specific flavors. By no means is this list inclusive. You need to build your own list of the attributes that are applicable to your situation, and the definitions that are meaningful to your tasters. If you set up a flavor profile, keep the number of attributes to a reasonable number. You're better off dealing with fewer attributes and doing the job well than trying to taste a whole range.

Glossary of Beer-Flavor Attributes

Fruity	Perfumy fruit flavor resembling apples.
Hoppy	Flavor due to aromatic hop constituents.
Bitter	Bitter taste derived from hops.
Malty	Aromatic flavor due to malt.
Hang	Lingering bitterness or harshness.
Tart	Taste sensation caused by acids, e.g. vinegar or lemon
Oxidized	Stale beer flavor. Resembles paperlike or

	cardboardlike flavor.
Grainy	Flavor of cooked cereal.
Medicinal	Chemical or phenolic flavor, at times resembling solvent.
Sulfur	Skunky -- odor of beer exposed to sunlight. Sulfur Dioxide -- taste/odor of burnt matches. Hydrogen Sulfide -- odor of rotten eggs. Onion -- reminiscent of fresh or cooked onion.
Bacterial	A general term covering off-flavors such as moldy, musty, woody, lactic acid, vinegar, or microbiological spoilage.
Yeasty	Reminiscent of yeast, bouillon, or glutamic acid.
Diacetyl	Typical butterlike flavor. The odor of cottage cheese.
Mouthfeel	Sensation derived from the consistency or viscosity of a beer. For example, thin or heavy.

These are some suggestions for definitions you might use when you first begin to develop a flavor profile.

I'd like to speak of the profiling system we use. It is not meant to be a standard, but it has been used successfully for many years. One of the first things that must be done is setting up an overall rating system. We use a nine-point hedonic scale, which runs from plus four to minus four, with zero being neutral.

9-Point Scale of Preference

+4 Like extremely
+3 Like very much
+2 Like moderately

+1   Like slightly
0   Neither like nor dislike
-1   Dislike slightly
-2   Dislike moderately
-3   Dislike very much
-4   Dislike extremely

I recommend being as descriptive as you can in your overall ratings to help your panels be as descriptive as they can.

Example of a Grading System to be Used in
Profile Evaluation of a Beer

+4   The highest mark the taster can give. A sound, clean beer that strikes the taster "just at the the right moment." A grade this high reflects strong personal preference.

+3   A sound, clean beer and one for which the taster shows some personal preference. These preferences, such as the correct hop character, excellent aromatic quality, etc., should be clearly stated, if possible.

+2   An average, sound, clean, salable beer. If the taster can find nothing wrong with the beer, it should receive a "+2" rating and one should suppress his personal likes and dislikes for a thin or heavy beer, bitter or sweet, etc.

+1   A sound, clean beer and one which has no abnormal faults, but the taster feels some normal tastes are a little more pronounced (too bitter, too sweet, etc.) or a little too subdued (less hop, less body, etc.) than generally found. A faint trace of a "normal" defect such as slight oxidation or a little too much of an SO_2 character is permitted.

0   A beer in which you can find nothing particular to praise and nothing particular to fault. It can have faults but not of an intensity to cause the taster to reject the beer. A neutral type of beer.

-1   A beer with some abnormal defects present but at a mild level. The taster does not like the beer, but does not seriously reject it. A beer that is stale or abnormally harsh or slightly light-struck or has a termo character belongs here.

-2   Abnormal defects present, such as diacetyl, termo taste, light-struck, can liner, medicinal, etc., at an easily detectable level, and the salability of the beer is questioned.

-3   Abnormal flavors present at a high intensity and probably cannot be eliminated by blending or the use of activated carbon. An objectionable beer.

-4   Undrinkable beer. You'll know it when you hit it.

The following is our actual taste profile and taste sheets. In tasting, we measure a total of thirty-five attributes, which might be a little too much for any-one. The first five at the top are all compulsory qualities. When the taster profiles the beer, he must evaluate those qualities and make a mark in the category, based on the plus or minus for the type and style of beer. For example, if he's tasting a lager beer, he'd judge it as an American lager. As such, it would be either staler or fresher than a normal lager beer; it would be thinner or fuller in body than a normal lager beer; etc.

The other compulsory marks are bitter and afterbitter,

found in the middle of the sheet. Again, those are rated on the average for each particular type of beer.

The taster mentally changes this scale when he profiles a malt liquor, an ale, or a European lager. Obviously you can't compare an American lager to another style of beer or a European lager. So the taster must shift gears.

Except for the seven attributes listed above, every attribute is a voluntary marking. If the taster gets an impression, he notes the intensity level from one to four, marking the dot that signifies the intensity. One dot is very mild, and dot four is very intense.

Every attribute that falls below "yeasty" on this chart is considered a negative attribute or a defect.

There is also a place to comment on hop quality, odor, and other properties. These are the taster's personal comments, made in addition to marking off the attributes and intensities.

The sheet should have a place for taster identification. We use a code, and date the sheet. We run three or four panels in a day, so we also indicate the panel and which side we tasted on.

This is an interesting point: we have ten tasters on our panel. We serve two packages of beer, so five people taste from each package. The obvious reason is that we can't get enough beer out of one package. The inobvious reason is that there is frequently package-to-package variation. It can be caused by high air in the package, for example. If we run into this situation, we have a re-taste to determine how serious the variation is.

We rate up to seven beers on a panel. Beyond that number, the acuity of the taster diminishes. On the taste sheet, each column represents a different beer. Please consult the sheet on page 125. If there are no markings

(24)   (1   2)   '3ICE   M4L   L15TE   6

	1	2	3	4	5	6
Identity (Brand)						
Lab. No.						
TALE, OXID. ←——→ FRESH						
hin ←— BODY ——→ full						
ess←—FLAVORFUL—→ more						
ARSH ←———→ SMOOTH						
ow←—HOP INTENSITY→ hi						
pecial Hop Quality?			NICE			
ODOR —→						
ROMATIC, winy, vinous						
Fruity, estery						
Spicy						
"Aley"						
"Alcoholic"						
ITTER, incl. non-hop						
Afterbitter						
SWEET						
Malty						
Caramel						
Syrupy						
RY						
Astringent/tart						
Husk, grainy						
Worty						
Sulfitic (SO$_2$)						
Sulfidic (H$_2$S, R-SH)						
YEASTY						
Light-struck, skunky						
Musty, cellar taste						
Woody						
Cardboard, papery						
Burnt, scorched						
Bready (past. taste)						
"Termo"/spoiled wort						
Diacetyl						
Acidic, sour (bact.)						
Metallic, inky						
FF, FOREIGN (Gen'l.)						
Phenolic						
OTHER PROPERTIES ?						
RATINGS	+2	+2.5	+3	+3	+2	-3.5

Copyright 1971

at the top, as in columns one, two, six, and seven, the beer is an American lager. As you can see, the beer in the third column is an ale, in the fourth a malt liquor, in the fifth a light beer. The brackets around columns one and two mean that tasters should specifically compare these two.

Normally, we drink the lighter beers first, moving on through to the heavier beers -- although on this taste sheet, it has been requested not to be that way.

All the compulsory categories at the top, and bitter and afterbitter, have been marked with circles or x's. The circles represent the average for that type and style of beer. The x's represent the plus or minus from that average. As I said, all other marks are voluntary, and are marked only if the taster notes these characteristics.

At the bottom is a numerical rating, which is the nine-point hedonic scale. Beer number one received a plus two, etc. That is the overall taste impression from that individual taster.

The sheet on page 127 looks like it is marked with hieroglyphics, but it does make sense. We take all individual taste sheets and mark them on this summary sheet. A summary sheet compiles the findings of the ten individual tasters. This particular sheet is marked for the first four beers on the previous sheet.

In looking at the attributes, if the taster's code appears alone, it means intensity one; with a line under it, it is intensity two; if it appears twice, it is intensity three; and if it appears twice with a line under it, it is intensity four. So we can see what taster said what about the beer, and to what intensity level. The numbers signify the total intensity levels.

TASTE PATTERN CHART (25)	LAGER A		LAGER B		MALT LIQ		ALE	
STALE, OXID. ◄──► FRESH	3	5	333 33 333	-8		+1	5	5
thin ◄── BODY ──► full		4	3 5	0	4 4 4	+3	44 4	44
less ◄─FLAVORFUL─► more	4 4 4 4	+4	4	+1	4 44 4	+4	44 4	444
HARSH ◄────► SMOOTH	3	5	3 3 3 3 3	-5	4	4	+2	4 4	4
low ◄─ HOP INTENSITY ─► hi	4			0		4	+1	44 4	44
Special Hop Quality							NICE	
ODOR ──►	SL. DULL		WORTY SOUR		ESTERY		NICE HOPPY ALEY	
AROMATIC, winy, vinous	T>OIA \S	15	T>OIAxt	14	T>OIAX\t S	18	T>OIAXtS	
Fruity, estery	T>OIAX\S	16	T>OIAx++	15	I>OIOG x\t$	20	T>OIAXtS	
Spicy	O	2	IOI	6	>OIOG	10	>OAX	
"Aley"							T>OAX\t	
"Alcoholic"					I>OAX\t	14	>OXI	
BITTER, incl. non-hop	T>OtAX\S	16	T>OIAx++	15	TI>IAX\tS	18	I>OIAX\tS	
Afterbitter	T>OIAX\S$	17	T>OIAx++	15	T>IAX\tS	18	IT>OIAX\tS	
SWEET	O	2			IX	4	>OG	
Malty	>OIAX	10	>IAX	8	OA XX	7	>OAXIS	
Caramel							OAXI	
Syrupy								
DRY							AXI	
Astringent/tart	>OIAX\	12	T>OIAXt	14	LV	4	AXS	
Husk, grainy			>OIA	8				
Worty			OVX	6				
Sulfitic (SO₂)					AX	4		
Sulfidic (H₂S, R-SH)								
YEASTY								
Light-struck, skunky								
Musty, cellar taste								
Woody								
Cardboard, papery			I>OIAX\S	16				
Burnt, scorched								
Bready (past. taste)			T>OIAX\S	15				
"Termo"/spoiled wort								
Diacetyl			>OAXS	10				
Acidic, sour (bact.)			>OAX	8				
Metallic, inky								
OFF, FOREIGN (Gen'l.)								
Phenolic			IOA	6				
OTHER PROPERTIES	CLEAN		CARD SPOILED		SL ALCOHOLIC		FLAVORFUL	

RATINGS	LAGER A				LAGER B				MALT LIQ				ALE			
	1	3	6	3	+25	1	-4	6	3	+30	1	4	6	3.5	+30	1	4	6	4
	2	1.5	7	2.5		2	-2	7	-2		2	3.5	7	3		2	3.5	7	3.5
	3	2	8	2	+2.5	3	-4	8	-2	-3	3	3	8	2.5	+3	3	4	8	3.5
	4	3	9	2		4	-2.5	9	-4		4	3	9	4		4	3	9	4
	5	3.5	10	2.5	9/0/0	5	-3	10	-3.5	0/0/0	5	2.5	10	3	10/0/0	5	3	10	3

J. E. SIEBEL SONS' CO., INC.
CHICAGO, ILL. - COPYRIGHT 1971

At the bottom are the overall numerical ratings, which are divided to get an average rating. For example, the first beer, Lager A, was rated plus 2.5, while Lager B was rated minus 3.

Of the other numbers beneath the circled one, the first indicates the number of panelists that responded positive, the second neutral, and the third minus. Lager A was rated ten positive, no neutrals, no negatives.

From this sheet, we can develop the flavor profile in a more readable, graphic form. Let's look at a sheet for Lager B on page 129.

The rating and panel distribution are marked in the bottom right corner, any comment is typed in, and the same scale of attributes is marked with a bar graph. The number that follows the bar graph is the total number of tasters who indicated that attributes.

You can easily see the high degree of negative comments below yeasty on this profile of Lager B. At the top, you can see a high degree of oxidation, which is further supported on the bottom by a fairly high-intensity reading on cardboard, papery, and bready, all tastes indicative of oxygenation. You also see that the tasters found diacetyl, acidic, and phenol, which are indicative of a biological defect.

One interesting use for a profile is laying one over another and judging your beer today to your previous months' production or judging it against competitors' beers. You can detect slight shifts in your profile, if there are any, which will allow you to take corrective action. Or if you want to modify your beer to another profile, you'll be able to see whether or not you've been effective.

Now take a look at page 131. This represents a com-

FLAVOR, O.K. ──── → FRESH
THIN ─── (body) ─── → FULL
LESS ←─ FLAVORFUL ──→ more
HARSH, RAW ──→ SMOOTH
low—HOP INTENSITY—→ high
AROMATIC, winy, vinous
Fruity, estery.
Spicy
"Aley"
"Alcoholic"
BITTER, incl. non-hop
Afterbitter
SWEET
Malty
Caramel
Syrupy
DRY
Astringent/tart
Husk, grainy
Worty
Sulfitic (SO_2)
Sulfidic (H_2S, R-SH)
YEASTY
Light-struck
Musty, cellar taste
Woody
Cardboard, papery
burnt, scorched
Bready, "pasteur. taste"
"Tormo" - spoiled wort
Diacetyl
Acidic, sour (bacterial)
Metallic, inky
Medicinal foreign, off

Lab. No.

Identity
Lager B

ODOR
Slightly sour

Any Special Hop Quality?

Other Properties

RATING

10 TASTERS

INCR. BITTERNESS
AFTER BITTER LINES

TASTE TEST

puterized flavor profile -- yet we're still dealing with the same taste sheet, the same attributes, and the same four-scale intensities.

Once the evaluation sheet has been turned in, the data is entered. Along the top of the sheet is the individual code for each of the ten tasters. If they make no response, a zero is entered; or if they do respond, the levels of intensity are marked with one, two, three, or four. At the bottom is the number the taster gave the beer, as well as an overall rating for the beer. So, simply and quickly, one can see the total intensity levels, which taster said what, the overall rating, the panel distribution, and at the bottom, any comments made by the taster.

From this sheet, the reviewer who is responsible for the final report will develop a final summary comment. He understands each individual taster's acuity. If someone is very sensitive to diacetyl, for example, he notes that and gives it more weight.

The next sheet on page 132 is even more visually explicit. The first figure shows the total intensity units (IU), followed by the number of panelists. It is a particularly good format for comparing profiles. At the bottom are the comments that have been drafted by the reviewer from the summary sheet.

Now I'd like to comment on the tasters themselves. In establishing the panel, make it a point to recruit people who have the time to serve. Tasters need to be available and need to take the job seriously. Next, orient them to what you expect of them, giving them the procedures, terminologies, profiles you use, etc.

Training is a very important in establishing the panel. You must familiarize your panelists with the various

Taste panel profile on Lager B   J.E. Siebel Sons' Inc.
Lab number : 222222
Initial Tasting,   Packaged July 16 ,1986,   Tested July 25 ,1986
Received July 24 ,1986

	t	c	o	l	d	a	x	z	w	s	Total
Stale<OXIDATION->Fresh	-1	-1	-1	0	-1	-1	0	-1	-1	-1	-8
Thin<----BODY----/Full	0	0	0	-1	0	0	1	0	0	0	+0
Less<-FLAVORFUL-->More	0	0	0	0	1	0	0	0	0	0	+1
Harsh<-PALATE-->Smooth	-1	0	-1	0	0	-1	0	-1	0	-1	-5
Low<-HOP INTENSITY->Hi	0	0	0	0	0	0	0	0	0	0	+0
AROMATIC, winy	2	2	2	2	0	2	2	0	2	0	+14
Fruity, estery	2	2	2	2	0	2	2	0	3	0	+15
Spicy	2	0	2	2	0	0	0	0	0	0	+6
Aley	0	0	0	0	0	0	0	0	0	0	+0
Alcoholic	0	0	0	0	0	0	0	0	0	0	+0
BITTER, incl. non-hop	2	2	2	2	0	2	2	0	3	0	+15
Afterbitter	2	2	2	2	0	2	2	0	3	0	+15
SWEET	0	0	0	0	0	0	0	0	0	0	+0
Malty	0	2	0	2	0	2	2	0	0	0	+8
Caramel	0	0	0	0	0	0	0	0	0	0	+0
Syrupy	0	0	0	0	0	0	0	0	0	0	+0
DRY	0	0	0	0	0	0	0	0	0	0	+0
Astringent	2	2	2	2	0	2	2	0	2	0	+14
Husk, grainy	0	2	2	2	0	2	0	0	0	0	+8
Worty	0	0	2	0	2	0	2	0	0	0	+6
Sulfitic (SO2)	0	0	0	0	0	0	0	0	0	0	+0
Sulfidic (R-SH)	0	0	0	0	0	0	0	0	0	0	+0
YEASTY	0	0	0	0	0	0	0	0	0	0	+0
DMS	0	0	0	0	0	0	0	0	0	0	+0
Light-struck, skunky	0	0	0	0	0	0	0	0	0	0	+0
Musty, cellar, woody	0	0	0	0	0	0	0	0	0	0	+0
Cardboard, papery	2	2	2	2	0	2	2	2	0	2	+16
Burnt, scorched	0	0	0	0	0	0	0	0	0	0	+0
Breddy, over pasteur.	2	2	2	2	0	2	2	2	0	1	+15
Termo/spoiled wort	0	0	0	0	0	0	0	0	0	0	+0
Diacetyl	0	2	2	0	0	2	2	0	0	2	+10
Acidic, tart	0	2	2	0	0	2	2	0	0	0	+8
Metallic	0	0	0	0	0	0	0	0	0	0	+0
Medicinal, phenolic	0	0	0	0	0	0	0	0	0	0	+0
Foreign, off	0	0	2	2	0	2	0	0	0	0	+6

Panel rating   -4.0 -2.0 -4.0 -2.5 -3.0 -3.0 -2.0 -2.0 -4.0 -3.5   -3.0
Distribution   0 / 0 / 10

Panelist	Hop qualities	Aroma	Other properties
t		worty sour	cardboard spoiled
c			
o			
l			
d			
a			
x			
z			
w			
s			

J. E. Siebel Sons' Company, Inc.

4055 West Peterson Ave, Chicago, Il 60646 (312) 463-3400

Initial Taste Profile

Lab Number : 222222	J.E. Siebel Sons' Inc.
Identity : Lager B	4055 W. Peterson Avenue
Package type :	Chicago, Il 60646
Packaging date : July 16 , 1986	
Date received : July 24 , 1986	Attn: Mr. Ted Konis
Date tasted : July 25 , 1986	

	Average
Stale<OXIDATION->Fresh	-8 IU
Thin<----BODY---->Full	0 IU
Less<-FLAVORFUL-->More	1 IU
Harsh<-PALATE->Smooth	-5 IU
Low<-HOP INTENSITY->Hi	0 IU
AROMATIC, winy	14 IU, 7 Panelists
Fruity, estery	15 IU, 7
Spicy	6 IU, 3
Aley	
Alcoholic	
BITTER, incl. non-hop	15 IU, 7
Afterbitter	15 IU, 7
SWEET	
Malty	8 IU, 4
Caramel	
Syrupy	
DRY	
Astringent	14 IU, 7
Husk, grainy	8 IU, 4
Worty	6 IU, 3
Sulfitic (SO2)	
Sulfidic (R-SH)	
YEASTY	
DMS	
Light-struck, skunky	
Musty, cellar, woody	
Cardboard, papery	16 IU, 8
Burnt, scorched	
Bready, over pasteur.	15 IU, 8
Termo/spoiled wort	
Diacetyl	10 IU, 5
Acidic, tart	8 IU, 4
Metallic	
Medicinal, phenolic	
Foreign, off	6 IU, 3

Panel rating: -5.0

Panel distribution : 0/ 0/10

Comments: Bacterial odor. Moderately oxidized. Harsh. Very estery and
          astringent. Rather diacaetyl-like, bacterial and grainy, slightly
          spicy and worty. Poor appeal.

tastes in beer, and explain words so everyone is speaking in the same terms. For example, they have to interpret "musty" as you do. Doctor a beer, let the panelists taste it, and then discuss it. Then later you can test to determine levels of acuity.

As odd as it might sound, tasting beer on a routine basis two and three times daily can become mundane. You have to keep your panelists motivated.

Performance is the key to good, successful tastings. You must monitor your panelists, and occasionally retest them to see that their acuities in different tastes have not diminished.

In selecting your panelists, choose people who are interested. If someone doesn't want to taste, don't force him into it. Health is pertinent. If the individual has allergies or health problems, he will not be able to taste as well as someone who is healthy.

As in beer, the best taster is consistent. He must be so accurate and consistent that he can duplicate results. You will find this out by doing periodic testing.

The panel should be held in a clean, quiet, well-lighted location. A cluttered office or a coffee room is not suitable. It should be pleasant, as the surroundings will definitely affect your tasters. It should also be convenient.

You certainly want a taste environment that is free from odors, as odors can have a residual effect. If there are lingering odors from cleaning solvents, tasters will not give accurate results.

One factor for consideration in setting up the panel is the color of the beer glasses. We at Siebel Institute use ruby red glasses, for example, because we don't want panelists to evaluate the physical characteristics of the beer -- i.e., the foam, clarity, color, etc. -- during tasting. during tasting, i.e., the foam, clarity, color, etc. They are there to taste, and taste only. Physical qualities are quantified in the lab.

Our panelists normally drink beers starting with the one on the left and moving toward the right. Therefore we place the lighter beers on the left, so tasters move from lighter to heavier progressively.

You should also give your panelists special instructions if there are any. We list them on a blackboard, rather than state them. There are also a few panel rules. We ask the tasters to refrain from making comments during the actual taste test. This includes smacking lips or retching. We also ask panelists to be on time to tastings, so that the test is not disrupted nor postponed.

Finally, no taster is allowed to change his marks once the test is over. When each panelist is finished, he lays the sheet down. When everyone has finished, they discuss the beer.

No matter how large or small your brewery is, you don't need expensive or complicated tasting equipment to conduct a valid tasting. In fact, you already have the most sophisticated instrumentation for tasting beer -- your own sense of taste and smell. The only problem in a smaller brewery is that you have fewer people to rely on for tastings. Perhaps you can exchange beers with someone for tasting, or periodically send your beers out.

The brewer should train himself to evaluate beer. If there is one thing I'd do in running a brewery, I'd get very proficient in identifying certain flavors, and particularly defect flavors. Then I could recognize them when they first occurred, hopefully in time to take action.

Finally, producing a high-quality beer, consistently, is the best thing you can do to ensure the sale of your beer.

Q: Do you use anything to neutralize taste between beers?

RS: No, we don't. A knowledgeable person sets up the beers, and he knows which should come first. You can have a carryover, but I don't favor nibbling on bread and crackers. If you have a carryover, you can retaste.

Q: What is the time frame for tasting?

RS: It takes fifteen or twenty minutes for trained people to taste six beers, including a five-minute concluding discussion.

Q: Are the beers poured at the same time?

RS: They are poured at the same time, and we strive for a certain temperature. Unless instructed differently, we normally serve the beers at about 45 degrees F.

Ron Siebel is president of J.E. Siebel Sons' company and is the fourth generation of his family to serve as the corporation president. He joined the company in 1966, after graduating from the University of Miami. In 1976, he graduated from the Siebel Institute and apprenticed at Molson's Brewery in Montreal, after which he worked in small U.S.breweries nationwide.

12. Brewers Always

Thomas Reap

Master Brewers Association of the Americas
Houston, Texas

On behalf of the Master Brewers Association of the Americas (M.B.A.A.), I extend my wishes for a successful meeting. From the sessions I've heard so far, this convention has been outstanding. It's very gratifying to listen to people tell it the way it is -- with no bull and no rose gardens. It helps us (large brewers) realize what the microbreweries are up against. From my position as Corporate Brewmaster at Anheuser-Busch, I am so accustomed to zero-zero-zero-zero on the end of every number that it' very difficult for me to exactly understand your dilemmas. The smallest brewery I ever worked in was 25,000 barrels, and we took it to 600,000 barrels in three years of expansion.

The conversations I've had in the past few days have led me to believe that many of you are in the planning stages of starting a brewing career. Therefore, you should be thankful to your colleagues who have laid it on the line to you. They've told you about the mistakes they've made so that hopefully you will not make the same ones.

Last night in my room I found two little chocolates on my pillow and a card. I'm sixty-three years old and have completed forty years in the brewing industry, so the words on the card seem particularly appropriate: "As I grow older, I pay less attention to what men say. I just watch what they do." These are the words of Andrew Carnegie.

With that, I'd like to cover the history of the M.B.A.A. I'm sure you are aware that the history of brewing dates back thousands of years. History records that the Babylonians and early Egyptians brewed a type of beer. As time progressed, brewing became an art. It is said that brewing is the second oldest profession in the world, although we won't discuss the oldest here.

From earliest recorded history until the 1880s, there was no actual recorded communication among brewers. During the 1880s, there were literally thousands of breweries in the United States ranging in size from extremely small, household operations to large plants -- a "large plant" being 100,000 barrels, compared to present-day large plants of 10 to 13 million barrels. (Our plant at Anheuser-Busch brewed 9.5 million of beer.) In the past, each brewery had its own brewmaster, but any research or development was either kept secret or passed on by word of mouth.

Realizing that brewers must intercommunicate in order to perfect and carry on the profession, a group of brewmasters started open discussions in around 1885 on methods to upgrade and share brewing information through a formal method. Thanks to their foresight, the groundwork was established for our profession as we know it today.

On 21 March 1887, about ninety brewmasters gathered in

Chicago to organize the Master Brewers Association of the United States. From the minutes of this first meeting, we find the following.

The objects for which it was founded are:

(a) to promote the mutual acquaintance of the members;
(b) to protect and further the interests of the brewing trade in every respect;
(c) to develop thoroughly, by an interchange of views, scientific questions relating to the brewing trade;
(d) to promote the training of brewers;
(e) to develop particular attention to the matter of apprenticeships;
(f) to foster and secure progress;
(g) to promote the development and protection of the brewing trade and its interests in the United States.

Other stipulations were that only German be spoken in the meetings and proceedings, and that the association be headquartered in Chicago. This is why even today the majority of the terminology used in our industry is derived from German, i.e., "lauter tun," "fassen," "Voescheissen," etc.

In October 1888, 229 people traveled to a convention in New York, of which 173 represented local districts. One important outcome of the meeting was the apprenticeship program.

Rules governing it were:

(a) it would be a two-year program;
(b) brewers who employed fifteen or more people would take two apprentices, and those with fewer than fifteen employees would take one; and

(c) at the completion of his two-year term the apprentice would be given an examination by his brewmaster, then be presented with a "Certificate of Graduation" upon recommendation of the association's board of directors.

During the years from 1888 to 1919, the Association was very active. It had a membership of over 2,000, was publishing its spokespiece magazine "Communications," and was sponsoring research projects on malt and brewing procedures.

From 1919 to 1933, the Volstead Act was in force (named for Andrew Volstead, the act forbade the sale of alcoholic beverages), but M.B.A.A. members stuck together. In 1933, the Volstead Act was modified to permit the brewing of 4 percent alcohol by volume (3.2 percent by weight) beers, and a M.B.A.A. convention was held in Chicago with revised bylaws. The name was changed to Master Brewers Association of the Americas, to include Canadian brewers.

The 1936 convention was held in Philadelphia and was dedicated to Louis Pasteur for his work.

From then to the present, much progress has been made. Here is where we stand today. We are an international organization with members from practically every country in the world. We have 400 members from Africa, 100 from South America, and many from the Caribbean, Europe, Japan, China, and other countries.

We have an annual scholarship award of $2,000 per year for people attending or entering a qualified university and majoring in studies relating to the brewing industry. Recipients do not need to be members of the M.B.A.A. nor be in the family of members. They must promise, however, that they will make every effort to work in the brewing industry when they graduate from school.

We sponsor and run a brewing-and-packaging course at the University of Wisconsin in Madison, Wisconsin. We also publish "Communications" and "Technical Quarterly," which consists of papers presented at our annual conventions. "Technical Quarterly" is one of the most sought-after publications in existence for people in the brewing trade and for various research groups in colleges.

We continue to sponsor research in malting and we update and publish the book *Practical Brewer*. We recently published a book on packaging.

The preceding is only a synopsis of the history and goals of the M.B.A.A. We recognize the increase in mini-breweries or microbrewers, especially in Canada and the U.S. We feel we have a lot to offer you, and you have a lot to offer us. Our doors are open for those of you qualify to become members of M.B.A.A. We presently have several microbrewers in our organization.

The duties and responsibilities of a brewmaster have not really changed much in the last hundred years; they have just become more sophisticated. We continue to deal with Mother Nature, and as you know, she rarely changes -- regardless of computers, automation, and advances in chemistry.

As a parting note from a brewmaster with forty years' experience, the secret word is "clean." When you feel certain that your operation is so-called "biologically clean," then clean it again, and you'll save yourself a great deal of trouble. Never install a piece of equipment until you know how to clean ev ery inch of it.

The purpose of the M.B.A.A. is communications. You are all welcome to attend our annual conventions and hear the latest papers presented and see thousands of square feet of exhibitions. I go out of office for the M.B.A.A. in October 1986, but if ever I can help any of you answer some of your questions, feel free to call on me. In large breweries or small, we are brewmasters first, last, and always.

Thomas Reap, president of M.B.A.A., has served at all levels of office in the M.B.A.A. Before he retired in 1985, he was Corporate Brewmaster at Anheuser-Busch, working for the brewery for twenty-six years. Early in his career, he apprenticed at the Eastside Brewery in Los Angeles (later Pabst) and attended the Siebel Institute of Technology in Chicago.

13. Getting Money for Expansion

James Brock

President, Koolau Brewing Company
Honolulu, Hawaii

My talk deals with how to raise funds for expansion. I approach this from the methodology that economic ventures operate according to rules; that venture management is a science, not an art; that management requires you to apply some general principles to specific events; and that from those principles, you can make very specific predictions about the future.

I believe that the forces in the microbrewing industry today are not ones we create ourselves. There has been a real change in the way people approach beer, and a real change in the way our economy and society are moving. These external forces are larger than all of us. The popularity of microbrewed products is not due to a marketing ploy. The shift towards quality beer is not because of something someone has done. Rather, I believe this trend is a change in the basic structure in the American society.

It is in response to these changes that we should be moving our industry. We should be trying to understand what has caused the American people to change their import patterns from 1 percent to 9 percent by volume in ten years. That didn't happen because of the people in this room, and it didn't happen because of marketing. It happened because of an external change in the system. Obviously, I differ from some of the others who have spoken here. My background is not in brewing, but primarily in engineering and representing investors.

Who Are You?

In trying to get funds for expansion, you must ask a series of questions about your brewery. First, what kind of firm are you? This will affect your ability both to expand and to raise funds. When we look at kinds of firms, we find they fall into five different groups. You can class them by sales or number of employees, but mainly I define them by management style.

Individual. Probably the smallest type of business is the individual. In this category, only one person does the work, although others may be involved. This single individual makes between $40,000 and $200,000 a year, and is limited in how much he can produce.

If you are running this kind of enterprise -- if you make all the beer, sell it, etc.-- you'll have a very hard time raising any money. You are unsuitable to investors, mainly because if you walk into the street and get run over by a truck, the business dies with you.

Mom/pop. These little enterprises are generally in the magnitude of $50,000 to $500,000. Usually the owners are doing the production, or directly supervising any employees, for lack of a professional-management structure. The owners are rarely trained in elements

considered necessary in business; for example, they are
not CPAs, professional managers, or marketers. But most
important, there is no delegation -- which brings us back
to the truck accident. If Pop gets runs over, the
business is gone.

Enterprise. This is a business with $500,000 to $5 million in sales. In this size business, there is a definite
distinction between owners and management, although the
separation is sometimes unclear. The major characteristic
here is the size and structure of the professional-management team.

Private Corporation. This size business usually has
from $3 million to $40 million in sales. But more importantly, it has a true separation between owners/
investors, management, and operations. The people who
produce do not manage, and the owners are usually third
parties. Yet, the managers know all the investors personally, and usually also know all the employees.

Public Corporation. This business has vertical as well
as horizontal separations. Investors and employees are
beyond the personal acquaintance of the managers. Here,
the process is dominant, not the people.

In our discussion today, we are focusing on the mom/pop
business, the enterprise, and the private corporation.
Between a mom/pop operation and an enterprise, there is
usually a large jump -- and that jump is signified by
professional management. The reason? You can't afford to
hire managers if you don't make enough money to pay them.
That's a major issue to investors.

What Do You Mean by Expansion?

The question here is, what kind of growth do you want?

There are three kinds of growth. One is when you **move from one category of business to another,** i.e., from a mom/pop business to an enterprise. Here the problem with finding an investor is that you are basically starting a new business when you move up, rather than growing. Then, you have to be able to prove to an investor that you can run an enterprise, based on your experience in a mom/pop operation.

The second kind of growth deals with the **transitions** in building a business. When you build, you go through a series of changes. In the beginning, you spend your time forming a concept. At this stage, you normally have seed investors.

Next, you have to prove your concept by constructing a model, developing a business plan, proving your market, selecting a site, finding your equipment cost, etc. Here you're raising venture money.

Next, you build your entity through implementation, meaning that you start manufacturing. Then, you go through a phase of debugging, of refining the process. Last, you normalize the business and your niche in the marketplace. This is when you stabilize sales.

This type of growth is not expansion; it should be an extension of your business plan, in which you anticipated your needs for money. If you go to a banker at this point saying that you've just started manufacturing beer and are out of money, don't hold out much hope for a check. That's not expansion, that's failure to predict the future. The banker is going to ask why you didn't know how much money you would need. You must enlist your investors in the beginning, not the end.

The third kind of growth is **true expansion.** Let's say that your enterprise is producing $3 million a year, and you have established your market. Now that your business is normalized, you want to expand to $5 million in sales. You're not going to change your management staff or style, you just want to add on. That's classical expansion.

The bad news is that money for expansion is very hard to find. You should have predicted your need in your business plan. More importantly, you should be able to fund your expansion out of your profits. If you're successful, you should be profitable. If you're not successl, then you shouldn't expand.

What Kind of Money Will You Raise?

Different businesses at times require different kinds of money -- money from different pockets. The first pocket is the **gambler.** He is interested in the gaming theory of making money. He might be someone willing to finance you with seed money, during the stage when you have only a concept. At that point, a roll of the dice determines whether or not he'll lose money on you.

The next person is the **speculator,** who is very similar to the gambler. He wants more than just good odds -- he usually wants a position in future gain. The issue for both the speculator and the gambler is the game. If you want to assess the ilk of an investor, ask about his previous investments. A gambler or speculator will tell you about the oil well. These people want a lot of return, and they want it as soon as the dice roll.

Venture capitalists and investors also have pockets with money in them. Venture people want to come into a business at a certain stage and get a piece of the action. Unlike the gambler, the investor doesn't want to take chances. He gives you the use of his money now, for a future gain. People often confuse investors with lenders, who are the last category.

A **lender** gives you the use of money now for a fee. The lender is the opposite of the gambler. Lenders take no risk. If you want to borrow money from them, you'd better have 120 percent security.

So before you ask for money for expansion, consider the different possible sources.

If you are a transition company, that is if you are evolving from one type of company to another, investors are very specific in their requirements. If you are in the individual category, as we discussed, you will not find money from any source, except from a relative who will loan you money on your personal value. The other exception is if you have sufficient security. Then you can use the security as collateral at a bank. But a gambler, speculator, or investor will not put money with the individual. Why? What would happen if you were so successful that you made $200,000 a year? His share would still be nothing.

A mom/pop operation is looked upon as being similar to that of an individual, and therefore hard to find money for. An investor wants professional management for his money. If you were to die, he'd have to hire someone to fill your place, but he couldn't do that for a business producing $500,000 a year. A decent professional controller costs $50,000 a year, plus the burden (office, trips, car, etc.). And that doesn't address the need for a brewmaster, general manager, and production manager -- the people who comprise the minimum team.

If you're a mom/pop organization, you're stuck with the extremes: gamblers and lenders. If you have no security, perhaps you can find someone who is relatively wealthy and will guarantee your bank loan. An exception are the Small Business Administration programs; but they will also want a personal guarantee.

If you do decide to go with a gambler, he'll ask if you're going to make the jump from being a mom/pop organization to being an enterprise. He'll ask, "Is there a chance that my 20 percent of your $750,000 business might grow to be 10 percent of a $5 million-a-year business?" If the answer is yes, good luck. If it's no, you won't be able to attract even a gambler. The point is, in both a mom/pop and an individual business, you have to qualify for the bank, or find a relative.

The enterprise is the hardest size business to raise money for. On one hand, the enterprise has a life of it's own, but on the other, it isn't large enough to pay professional managers. It is usually a mom/pop business that has tried to make the jump. (Note that I said "jump." Mom/pop businesses don't evolve from twelve to fifteen employees; they jump from twelve to thirty.) But the banks still treat it as a mom/pop business.

If you want an acid test of whether you're an enterprise or a private corporation, find out whether your bank would require a personal guarantee from you. If it would, you're an enterprise, and the bank looks to you for response. It sees no separation between the owners and the managers. If you're a private corporation, however, the bank sees the business as an entity in itself and doesn't require a personal guarantee. Your business is then big enough that if one of the managers were to be run over by a truck, he could be replaced.

It's around the $3 to $5 million range that you can look for money from true investors -- those who are willing to give you money for future gain. Smaller organizations require a tremendous amount of faith from investors. But you may be able to raise money for a smaller business if you have a good track record, or if you have an angel with a good track record.

In a public corporation, lenders are the money source. The New York Stock Exchange is essentially a lending institution. Public corporations don't pay enough return to interest a venture capitalist.

Where Will You Find Money?

The next question is, how can you interest investors? I've already spoken about different kinds of money: gamblers will take risks with you, investors defer profits, and lenders want a fee. Your ability to raise money from any source is basically contingent on one thing: your ability to leverage is directly related to how strong your future cash flow will be -- not the past, but the future. If you can't show projections for cash flow to investors, you won't get money, unless you have enough security.

Of all the money sources I've defined, a mix is the best. For example, in the initial stages of Koolau Brewery we needed $3.6 million, plus in the first year of production we need an additional $1 million in capital. About $400,000 in risk money was raised through a general partner corporation. We then raised $750,000 through a limited partnership. That gave us about $1.2 million. The additional money had to be raised through lenders, by securing the real estate ($2 million) and by securing the equipment.

The lenders wanted a set fee, paid every month, whether

or not we make a profit. The limited partners got advantages because of tax credits. The investors who put in the original seed money receive a larger piece of the equity. So we combined the speculator with the investor with the lender. Almost any enterprise requires some combination of these three sources.

The last point I'll stress is that you should be aware of the acquisition cost of money. My experience is that any money you find will cost between 10 and 20 percent. Even a bank, when all the front costs are added up, charges at least 10 percent. Remember that you'll also pay for attorneys, CPAs, your time in making the presentations and any up-front fee. Budget into your plan that you'll spend 10 percent on the cost of money.

When you decide what kind of firm you are, how much money you need, and what kind of money you need, research where to find it. The lending institutions are easy to find. Finding gamblers, unless you know them personally, is more difficult, and you may even have to pay a fee of 30 percent to find them. You can pay the fee in several different ways.

First, you can hire someone to do it for you. If you have no experience in raising money, I suggest that you seriously consider this. Even though my business is representing investors, Koolau Brewery was the first venture I put together on my own account. I can tell you that raising money for myself was one of the most painful things I have ever done. In $25,000-chunks, putting together that $1.2 million was not a chore I'd like anyone to have to go through. So smile as you pay the professional money raiser 12, or 15, or 18 percent. Believe me, it's cheap!

But don't pay anyone the fee up front. There are people

who want a $10,000 retainer. Or they'll ask you to sign a contract requiring payment even if you raise the money yourself. Make sure you agree to pay a fee only upon performance, and that you pay only for your own consulting, attorney, or accountant fees. If the the money finder is reputable, he will not require the fee up front. If he asks for it up front, run -- don't walk -- out of the office. A 15 to 20 percent fee is not unusual, but it is paid at the end, not the front.

Differentiate between money raising and consulting. If you don't know how to structure your operation or write a business plan, you need a consultant, not a fund raiser.

This may all seem very negative to you. I realize that in the microbrewing business, people have begun or are looking at starting smaller enterprises. They speak of projections of $500,000 to $750,000 a year. My reaction is that the negative view is realistic. If you are moving from being an employee, you may think it is a big jump to go from $50,000 to $700,000 a year. But in the real world, that's not a very big business, and won't be considered a real business in most situations. You can't hire professional managers, and if you can't hire professionals, you are doing your own thing, not building a business.

So far as specifics, your best bet in finding local sources for money is your bank. Ask questions like "Who do you know in this town who has put together ventures?" "Are there people here who guarantee loans for a fee?" "Is there a local development corporation who can borrow money from the SBA?"

In finding money, you must appraise two assets: tangible versus intangible. Your tangible assets -- your equipment and real estate -- should justify lenders. Your intangible assets -- your knowledge -- should justify investors.

Q: The businesses you're talking about are bigger than most microbreweries. But is it realistic for a microbrewery to start out so big?
JB: I'm not making a judgment that mom/pop business are good or bad. I'm trying to define the reception you'll get in the financial community. If you're not large enough to have professional management, if you're not large enough to have a business that stands on its own, you'll have a difficult time finding money. Your sources of money in this country are severely limited. I don't know an answer.

Breweries are very capital intensive, and if you don't have a source of money to pay for basic startup, you're in the wrong industry. You may take what I say negatively, but if you've been out trying to raise money, you'll see that what I'm saying is true. The brewery industry is odd, because a brewery is classified like the corner grocery or a restaurant depending on gross sales.

Q: If you're up in the $5-million range, you'll be head-to-head with the big boys.
JB: Yes, then you have to define your niche -- whether it's a unique beer, or a unique marketing area. In Honolulu, we're focusing on producing a fresh beer, while every other beer comes 2,500 miles. Without a unique identity, without a reason for existing in the first place, it's questionable that you should be in business.

Q: But you can find a niche for less than $1 million a year.

JB: Yes, you can. But can you convince investors that you have a viable business that will survive five years of business, or a divorce, or your death? Below $750,000 a year, it's difficult. It's got to big enough to have a professional manager to make that investor comfortable. But I'm not saying that you can't run a very successful business at every one of the above-mentioned levels.

James Brock is president and CEO of Koolau Brewing Inc., in Honolulu, Hawaii. He is also the president of Honolulu Consulting Group, a management services corporation. Prior to developing HCG, he was president of Brock and Associates, an engineering consulting firm. He has lectured at the University of Hawaii and the Asian Technical Institute on theory of design and strategic-planning future studies practice.

14. Marketing vs. Public Relations

Daniel Bradford

**Marketing Director, Association of Brewers
Boulder, Colorado**

The subject of publicity, public relations, promotions, and reactions is quite a broad subject. I'll outline some terms, then give you some basic ideas for strategies in the hopes that by the end of my talk, you'll have a grasp of the public-relations-minded attitude. With that attitude, you can begin looking for your own opportunities.

My assumption for this talk is that you have small-to-nonexistent advertising budgets, you have special, unusual products with a certain amount of talkability, and you have personality behind your products. I emphasize that last point. The large brewers do not have the personality behind their product that we do, if we cultivate it.

We're working here with four different concepts. To define terms: publicity isn't advertising. **Publicity** is media attention to a specific angle, event, or circumstance. **Public relations** is radically different than publicity, and is what most microbrewers are woefully lacking. Public relations is the ongoing positioning of the company within the market.

The third element is promotion, which most microbrewers have down pat. It includes balloons, ties, horses, etc. **Promotion** is defined as visibly interjecting the company image, personality, and products into the community.

The fourth element, which I think is totally overlooked in nonadvertising, is reaction. **Reaction** is your response to local and national stories and events. Having a good reaction is the result of an extended publicity campaign. By that I mean that if anything is happening in the media that has to do with beer, small business, quality, or lifestyle, then you want reporters calling you to get your opinion. You become an "informed source."

Why do we involve ourselves in publicity, promotions, public relations, and reactions? Because they have credibility. Anyone with money can buy an ad. But people who read advertising discount its credibility because it was paid for. News stories, on the other hand, tend to be bad news. The public relations angle, however, bridges the information gap between advertising and news. For example, this conference has been on the television stations in Portland (Oregon) three times already. It took me two weeks to make that happen, but the effect is that the people who see the television spot believe this conference is credible.

Microbrewers face a few problems. For one, we are dealing with a different market than existed a few years ago. There are a lot of microbrewers now, and the newness of being a microbrewer may not be good enough to get you on the news. Also, the industry is starting to get confused about what constitutes a microbrewery, contract brewery, or small-scale commercial brewery. Years ago, *U.S. News and World Report* listed only five microbrewers, and of those, only two were actually micros. Microbreweries are also growing into regional breweries, which is adding to the confusion. Besides that, imports are becoming more aggressive, and microbrewers are becoming more competitive among themselves.

On the other side of the coin is a gold mine. Consumers are getting very well educated about quality beer, and it is not as hard to sell our beer now as it was five years ago. People understand quality, now. The media is also getting well informed. I have a mailing list of 1,2000 media across the country, and of that, 15 percent are totally up to speed on the renaissance in American brewing.

Also, the beers are getting much better. Now, micro-brewed beers are consistently a treat, and therefore much easier to sell. The story of beer is developing in complexity and is a nicer story to tell. "The making of beer": it has a nice ring to it. Further, beer is the third most popular beverage, and microbrewery markets are becoming very well targeted.

Those are the strengths and weaknesses. Now how are we going to make our attention-grabbing program work? First, one excellent sales tool is **personality.** We have three elements of that concept: beer, brewer, and brewery. All three are very easily sold as personalities. For example, one Denver distributor built a whole story around Sierra Nevada's Bigfoot in his sales routine.

The brewery also has a salable personality. Here in Portland, Fred Bowman has his tasting room in Portland Brewing Company, building in the character of the brewery. Of course, the brewer himself has a salable personality. The character of the brewer should be played up to media as a sales tool. Coors Brewery has done a remarkable job of presenting the people in their brewery to

the public. Jim Koch of Boston Beer Company and Matthew
Reich of Old New York Brewing Company are also doing excellent job of presenting themselves.

Customer loyalty -- and not brand loyalty -- is another
element of sales Heretofore, the brewing community has
focused on brand loyalty. This is dramatically changing.
Now we're going after people loyalty. We want customers
to be loyal to our brewery, our products, our personnel,
our way of life, and our attitude. We're now trying to
tie people into who we are and what we're doing. We do
this by transforming words and taste into some sort of
image -- a feeling -- about our brewery. Take, for example, the brewing community in Portland, Oregon. Brewers
here have created a community that they're selling to
their customers.

Community base is an element I don't see worked very
often. Most breweries are local breweries; as such, they
owe an allegiance to their community. Constant interac-
tion with the community through charities, special
events, parades, etc., can give you an excellent
opportunity for public relations. But don't make the
mistake of expecting the community to come knocking on
your door for these events; you have to go out and find
events to participate in.

Strategies

I'd like to cover some strategies for enacting each of
these four elements. The whole idea behind public relations is effective communication with staff, distributors, investors, and the interested public. I tend to
view public relations as your in-house vehicle. You want
to keep your people happy, and you do that by finding out

what they need and working to provide it.

Among the tools for doing this is an annual report. If you have to do an annual report, you can turn it into an elegant tool. Even if you're not publicly held, an annual report is still a good idea. Another idea is to make sure you tell everyone involved about company changes. People like to know what's going on, and if they hear it from you, rather than someone else, it's a plus in your favor.

Publicity is the art of building positive consumer awareness and affection through creating media attention around specific events. I believe most of you are good at this, but things to consider are comparative tastings, special brews, and creating a tradition. Everyone knows about Oktoberfest. How about creating your own annual special beers?

Reaction is the skill in building community support through acknowledgment as a responsible and reputable member of the community. I can't overemphasize the community linkage for publicity, public relations, promotions, and reactions. For example, join a community organization against drug traffic. Once you're plugged into that, you may be called as an expert by a newspaper when the issue of drunk driving comes up. Then you can present the brewers' side.

One angle underused by brewers is using your pursuit of excellence in manufacturing a quality product to gain media attention. You're focusing so much on good beer, that you haven't stepped back to look at the fact that you're producing an incredibly good product. Get that fact out!

Another angle is civic pride and booster activities. For example, Boulder Brewery built a facility its community can be proud of. The building is noticeably outstanding. You may not be planning to build a new building, but you can build a reputation as being an ambassador for your community. By all means, join the local Chamber of Commerce.

There is one downside to this, however. Don't get too identified with a stance or position. The Coors brothers have had problems with that in the last fifteen years, even to the point of having misquotes attributed to them. So in giving your reactions, steer clear of social issues, and keep your response generic.

Handling the Print Media

Let me run through a few general principles for handling newspaper reporters.

- Make friends with people you don't have to. In this business it helps if you're a schmoozer — that is, if you cultivate friendships.
- Remember that you're doing a reporter a favor when you give him a story.
- Reporters need news, and you need reporters.
- Be sensitive to reporters' deadlines and give them good facts.
- Always give reporters access to the people in your company.
- Don't ever stonewall on a question you can't answer. Get back to reporter with the facts they need once you find them out. And don't ever lie; it will get back to you.
- Get with the right reporter at the local newspaper. Target your press releases and keep your PR short.
- PR has to be news and not PR, or you're wasting your time.

Everyone likes to go to lunch, except reporters. If you have a brewpub that serves food, ask a reporter or editor over to your place for lunch. But often reporters are so busy, that it's better for you to visit them in the office. Develop a few good relationships with the editors who have some clout. Don't always try to sell them something; just get to know them. Then they'll call you when they need something.

The downside of the print media is that the press is sometimes unrestrained, and prints what it wants. So be careful in what you say. Be thorough, keep it simple, and repeat it five, six, seven times. Also be aware that reporters have quirks and may slant a story according to their quirk.

There are different departments in the newspaper that you can approach with an appropriate story about your brewery. "Features" editors are looking for stories with a long shelflife, because features may be worked on for a couple of weeks. One angle for a feature is beer history. Make some solid connections between your brewing and brewing in history.

"Lifestyle" editors want human interest or something that reflects a fad or trend. For example, people are drinking less beer, but better beer; or more women are beer lovers.

"City Desk" covers fast-breaking news with a one-day shelflife. This might include the bottling of your 100,000th bottle, a dozen visiting German brewers, or the fact that you're exchanging brewmaster with a brewery in Europe.

The "Business Section" is your bread-and-butter for communicating with the business community. Strive to get into this section. Most of you will eventually have

financial, marketing, and distribution problems as you
evolve. Although a lot depends on your bank balance,
whether or not the business community comes to your support depends on your good public image.

The "Sports Section" may seem like a fairly unlikely
place for you at first glance, but if you sponsor a run,
a tennis match, or soccer team, you can get your name out
in front of people on a consistent basis.

Photographs are an important element for print. Use
them frequently. Photos that are 5-by-7-inch and
black-and-white are best for newsprint. If you're approaching magazines, send color slides -- not prints.
Photos should tell a very simple story that's easily
grasped. Don't be afraid of using props such as a sprig
of wheat, lederhosen, a brewer's paddle, etc. Or use two
people doing an activity. Standing in front of a fermentation vessel with your arms crossed really doesn't get
it. Showing a photo of someone awarding a plaque may be
all right for a trade journal, but it won't make it in a
newspaper.

Considerations for Different Media

The most important factor in dealing with different
media is deadlines. Stay away from daily reporters in the
afternoon and stay away from food-section people on Tues-
day.

Local television stations have a very short lead time.
They'll put whatever you send them in a file, then take
it out the day they're going to use it. In sending a
press packet to television, try to communicate some image
or drama. Television is looking for action. Using
celebrities for bottling, delivering a case of beer to

the governor, etc. would convey an image you're looking for.

Radio announcers love phone interviews, so have some background noises from bottling or brewing going while you're talking. Analyze the schticks of local talk-show hosts in your area to see where you fit in, and keep them supplied with a couple of your latest beers. Don't waste any time on Sunday morning public service announcements or 3 a.m. talk shows.

Community cable is still up for grabs, but I think it's worth cultivating some contacts there. You can probably get on a talk show, and you might even get a feature story.

In considering the usefulness of the media, remember that ratings are used to sell advertising. They do not reflect listeners' or readers' willingness to act on a message. Exposure on the MacNeil-Lehrer show did not produce one new customer for one of my clients. But identical coverage in two competing newspapers produced completely different reactions for another client. So analyze the media, and rely heavily on your subjective opinions.

Sales Tools

How do you create sales tools? The biggest is the **press package.** Start with a good lead, writing in very clear style. Start with the main point and develop it in two-sentence paragraphs. You must tell a good story. Close the story with background data, such as the style of your beer, age of your brewery, brewery capacity, etc. Press releases should be one to six pages, and should convey a well-developed idea.

Next add a tip sheet. Use this to present relevant story ideas that directly or indirectly support the lead story: the newness of the microbrewing industry, the renaissance of handcrafted beers, the effect of micros on the brewing industry, etc. Include coasters, samples, labels, etc. that will perk up the readers' interest.

The third element is the fact sheet. Load this up with related statistics on beer. And finally, include biographies of relevant individuals. Close with names, addresses, telephone numbers of associated people, such as Philip Katz of the Brewer's Institute, Howard Kelly of Modern Brewery Age, or Charlie Papazian and myself of the Institute for Fermentation and Brewing Studies.

What you want to do is build a press package that makes it really easy for the reporter to act on a story idea.

Press meetings are virtually dead. I rarely use these unless something is really hard to sell. If you're going to attempt this, you had better have a really good story. Invite the key, target people, and be sure to have food and beer. Be sure of your participation: there is nothing worse that a press party that no one attends.

What I call the **hot lead** is a favorite stunt. If you have a one-shot activity, give reporters or television a quick phone call. They may or may not take you up on it.

Keep a photo file. People tend to underestimate the value of having a complete photo file of your products and personnel. It's an invaluable tool. Keep multiple copies of up-to-date photos on hand so you can send them to newspapers, etc.

The most underrated element of public relations is the **company spokesperson:** you have to have one. If your company is small, all your employees should be prepared to talk to the media about your brewery. I know you may be gun-shy, but stay in control. You are the expert; you know about your company. Use your comprehensive knowledge to your advantage by expressing the salient points succinctly, avoiding digressions, representing yourself as the best authority, and avoiding loaded questions.

Display items such as table tents and posters, and promotionals such as t-shirts, are almost impossible to judge the value of. Their purpose is to create image recognition, but I think most of the items are old-hat.

In staging a **promotional campaign,** sit down and decide your goals, then tie your campaign into an appropriate media and department. Is it best for newspaper, radio, or television? Do you want to do a slow-burn or an across-the-board campaign? Once you decide, build your tactics, time table, press packet, targeted audience, etc. Follow each contact repeatedly. First call and ask which person should receive your packet. After you send the press release, call that person and ask how you can help.

Evaluate your publicity campaigns in terms of your sales goals. Which work best for you? Be realistic. How much can you expect from a public relations, publicity, or promotional campaign?

Repeat coverage is more important, in my opinion, than sales because it will develop your position in the community. Once you get one good story, you're likely to get another. Strive for name recognition; this is when the newspaper calls and asks my opinion on a related subject.

My last point is that once you begin a public relations or promotional campaign, you can't just slip in and out of it. It takes concerted, repeated effort. When you have made the commitment to your community, you can't fall back on it. Happy hunting.

Daniel Bradford is marketing director for the Institute for Fermentation and Brewing Studies and the Great American Beer Festival, both divisions of the Association of Brewers. He is also a free lance promotionalist.

15. Contract Brewing

Matthew Reich
Old New York Brewing Company

James Temple
Smith and Reilly Brewing Company

Alan S. Dikty
Hibernia Brewing Company

Alan S. Dikty (Eau Claire, Wisconsin)

Let's begin with a definition: contract brewing means that an individual or company contracts with a brewery to produce a specific beer just for that individual or company. This is different than private label, wherein the individual or company contracts with a brewery to take one kind of beer and put the individual's or company's label on it. Private label has been common for a long time, but contract brewing is fairly recent, growing as the microbrewery industry has grown.

There are three advantages contract brewing offers to potential new brewers. The first is that you don't have to build a brewery to get your beer on the market. Many of you are thinking of opening a microbrewery, but the problem is that to do so, you must commit a large sum of money for a long time before the first case of beer is ready. Further, you don't know if the beer you're going to produce is going to sell. Contract brewing provides a reasonable method of test marketing.

Second, because you are not concerned with the day-to-day production of your beer in contract brewing, you can concentrate on test-marketing. You don't have to be in the brewhouse every morning at 5 a.m. to fire up the mash tun, which gives you time for sales.

Finally, with a few exceptions, few of you have unlimited resources. By being able to concentrate time and money on marketing rather than production, you may have a better chance for establishing a viable product in the marketplace.

On the other side of the coin, there are several reasons why contract brewers are interested in brewing other people's beer. It provides them with a contribution towards overhead. When you have a brewery, the meter runs twenty-four hours a day, so the more production you turn out, the lower your total overhead cost is. A contract brewer also likes the profit he makes on a product that is already bought and paid for, rather than sitting on the supermarket shelf.

Contract brewing does have its drawbacks for new brewers, however. Obviously, if you contract brew, you have your beer, but not a brewery. Many microbreweries emphasize their localness, which you can't do if your beer is being produced several hundred miles away.

Another drawback is that most breweries require a minimum production. Some breweries won't look at you unless you are willing to commit in advance to 100,000 cases.

Our panelists are Matthew Reich and James Temple. Matthew is the owner of Old New York Brewing Company (New York City), which began as a contract brewery, brewing through the F.X. Matt Company in Utica, New York. He has achieved what many contract brewers are dreaming of: he established enough of a market for his product to build a brewery.

Jim is from Smith and Reilly (Vancouver, Washington), which started as a contract brewer and is content to remain so. Smith and Reilly's beer was originally produced under contract in by Lucky Lager and then by Olympia. Smith and Reilly began as a draft operation and expanded to bottles, which has resulted in a jump in sales.

James Temple

The first thing you have to do is to convince a distributor to take your beer. That is one of the biggest problems any specialty beer has. Most distributors are unwilling or only marginally interested in carrying a specialty beer, and it takes a lot of effort to convince them you have a good, viable beer they can make a profit on.

By contract brewing, we basically had a built-in distribution network right from the beginning. Distributors don't want to order in a quantity that makes shipping worthwhile to anybody. Yet, if a distributor 200 miles away calls and orders three kegs of beer, you have to supply him. It's a major headache.

But if you can tie into the network of the brewery making your beer, as we did with Lucky Lager, the ease in shipping becomes phenomenally simple. That is, in itself, the major advantage in contract brewing. When someone wants our beer, it is put on the back of a truck that is already going there.

The third advantage relates to the cost of your beer. We wanted to make a European-style lager, instead of an ale. But to compete, we couldn't charge $6 or $7 a six-pack, or $60 or $70 a keg. We had to be more in the

Canadian price range -- $4.79, $4.99, $5.19 a six-pack or
$40 to $50 a keg. If we had spent $1.5 million building a
microbrewery, we'd have had to raise the cost of our product out of the range where we could successfully sell
it.

A disadvantage to contract brewing is the big brewery
mentality. Olympia, who now makes our beer, has expectations for a certain quantity -- and they are used to volumes with lots of zeros.

Another disadvantage is that the brewmaster has very
definite ideas about how to brew beer, and he may not
want to brew a certain kind of beer in his brewery. For
this reason, we've had to compromise between the beer we
wanted to make and the beer he's willing to make. Fortu-
nately, Olympia has bent over backwards to accommodate
our recipe, particularly in the transition from Lucky
Lager. Olympia wasn't willing, however, to allow us to
bring our Lucky Lager yeast into the plant. Naturally,
the flavor of our beer changed at that point.

Contract beers are the orphan child of the beer industry. No one knows what to do with them. What are they?
Specialty beers, superpremium beers, big brewery beers?
When Smith and Reilly first began, we thought long and
hard about how we fit into the industry. At that point,
we felt it would be difficult to go into the trade as a
contract beer, considering the consumer education that
would be necessary, and we were initially lumped with the
boutique beers. But we felt we had the same commitment
that microbrewers have.

Now as the market has grown and more people are familiar with specialty beers, we have come out and said
that we are a contract brew. We have the best of both
worlds; we have all the advantages a big brewery offers

in quality control, and yet we have all the advantages of being a small brewery in the personal care we take with our products.

Matthew Reich (New York City)

I'm probably not a good person to have on this panel. I'm such a cynic about contract brewing, now that I have my own brewery. Before I had a brewery in New York City, I would eloquently defend contract brewing, but now I think it's basically consumer fraud. If you can get away with it, great!

There are a lot of problems with contract brewing. The first is that you are constrained in packaging, brewing, and ingredient selection by the brewery you use. You can't use your own yeast. We always bought our own hops, and our own malt, but most places won't let you do that. F.X. Matt Brewing Company, where we brewed beer for the last four years, has some wonderful people. It is a spotlessly clean brewery that makes phenomenally good beer, so we were lucky, but there were problems nevertheless. For example, their labeling machine would only take one size label, and we couldn't use private molded glass because we had to use stock glass the brewery could run on their filler.

When I started, there weren't any other contract brewers. I believe I originated the concept when I went to the BATF six years ago. They wouldn't even let me put "Brewed under license" on my label. I had to put "Brewed by the F.X. Matt Brewing Company for the Old New York Beer Company." BATF insisted that the Matt name went on the top line of the mandatory label and our name was on the second. Today, this has changed. The BATF has obviously become more liberal on labels.

The fact is, there are a lot of private-label beers, and whether or not they are contract brewed is a thin line of definition. In New York City, there are five or six private label malt liquors available from a couple of brewers on the East Coast. There are also three or four private label maltas, a nonfermented, sweetened wort sold to Hispanic consumers.

A big problem, of course, is that after you leave the big brewery who is brewing your beer and build your own, how can you duplicate the flavor? We've come pretty close, but we've spent over $4 million on our brewery where we have some very, very good chemists and brewmaster. We didn't skimp on any money.

In New York, people really don't care whether or not we're a local brewery. New Amsterdam could be brewed in Germany as far as they're concerned. You can go into a bar and ask, "Hey, did you know there's a brewery in New York City?" The answer will be, "Yeah, it's Rhinegold." That brewery left New York City in 1976.

One other problem is that the brewery making your beer may go out of business. You are totally at the whim and mercy of the vagaries that affect your brewer. Most brewers in the U.S., with the exception of Anheuser-Busch and Heileman, are not terribly stable business entities and are subject to many pressures. They may be sold and the new management may not want to be in the contract brewing business. As a contract brewer, you don't control your business and could find yourself without any beer.

Neither do you have any jurisdiction over the quality control in the brewery making your beer. If it gets a bacterial infection, the spoilage organisms may get into your beer. You don't have your own lab technician there, and even if supply your own ingredients, you purchase in such small quantities that you cannot control the quality.

The benefit of contract brewing is that it takes very little initial investment, and you can make a lot of money on contract brewing. Sometimes I wonder why we bothered to spend $4 million when we used to be a profitable little company. Now, it's a tremendous cash drain.

Q: How about building your brewery and also contract brewing?
Alan Dikty: This is already happening. Some brewers find they can afford to build the brewery, but cannot afford the bottling equipment. They can then either be a draft brewery or a brewpub. It's a reasonable compromise, because a bottle shop is a very expensive proposition.

Q: What are the costs of start-up bottling at a contract brewer?
Alan Dikty: There are two factors: one is the sales and marketing costs of selling a bottled beer, and the other is inventory. Most contract brewers require you to purchase the custom package for your beer -- labels, six-pack carriers, mother cartons, custom bottlecaps, etc. The cost is variable, but you will certainly have lay in supplies for more than just your initial trailer load. Anything that has your name on you have to pay for.
Matthew Reich: We raised $255,000 to start with, and it was very, very tight. For the first seven or eight months, I took home only enough money to live on. It helps to raise $500,000.

Q: It is my feeling that contract brewing can be an extremely dangerous threat to the microbrewing industry of the U.S. What do you think about the future of contract brewing? Everyone in this room could become a contract brewer within a month. I think there's a real question of integrity.

Alan Dikty: While I recognize the potential for glutting the market, I don't think that point will come for quite awhile. There are many, many people who don't know about microbrewed beers.

Matthew Reich: I don't consider myself a microbrewer, and I don't consider myself part of any movement. I'm a brewer, I'm selling consumer product, and the goal is to get consumers to buy my product and build a consumer base. My competition is not just another microbrewer or import, it's every other beer on the shelf. I don't think it matters whether a brewer has his own production facility. Success has to be measured by economics, not by the ideology of whose beer is better.

I think that the only reason to build a facility is if you love it. I love to walk in and smell boiling wort. I believe that our brewery will grow much, much larger, but the additional investment won't necessarily be in production facilities, but in marketing.

Matthew Reich is the creator of the Old New York Brewing Company. He graduated with honors from the University of Massachusetts in business and economics and worked at Citibank and Hearst Corporation before founding his brewery.

Alan Dikty is vice-president and director of product development for Hibernia Brewing Ltd., brewer of numerous contract and private label beers, besides its own brands.

He began in the brewing business as an industry researcher.

James Temple is vice-president with Smith and Reilly. He graduated from the University of Oregon, and has been with Smith and Reilly for more than two years.

Brewers Publications Books

Beer and Brewing, Volume 6

Beer and Brewing is absolutely useful to professional brewers! Here is info from brewing experts at Siebel, Anheuser-Busch, Anchor Brewery, Coors Brewery, and others. In June 1986, 20 brewers and educators spoke at the National Homebrew Conference. This is a transcription of those talks -- complete with original charts and graphs.
5 1/2 x 8 1/2, 256 pp., illus., softcover $18.95

Brewing Lager Beer

This is the most comprehensive book on decoction mashing that we've seen. Part 1 examines beer ingredients. Part 2 guides you through planning and brewing seven classic lager beers -- including recipes. Brewer's tables of info are excellent.
5 1/2 x 8 1/2, 320 pp. index, illus., softcover $12.95

Brewing Mead

Can mead be sold to the American public? Our guess is yes, just as it is in Australia. Meads legendary history is a superb marketing tool. Here are step-by-step recipes and instructions for making this honey-based brew. And its history is included.
5 1/2 x 8 1/2, 208 pp. illus., softcover $9.95

Microbrewers Resource Handbook and Directory

Here are the names, address, and phone numbers of the brewing industry, plus a planning guide for starting and operating a brewery. Every brewer and supplier will find the data in this directory worth every cent of its price.

MRH also lists the step-by-step process of starting a micro-or pub-brewery from concept to finished beer.
8 1/2 x 11, 146 pp., illus. $35.00

Shipping is $2.50 per order.
Call in your Credit Card order now to 303-447-0816.
or make check payable to: Association of Brewers P.O. Box 287, Boulder, CO 80306-0287